OSPREY
MILITARY

POLTAVA 1709

GENERAL EDITOR DAVID G. CHANDLER

OSPREY MILITARY **CAMPAIGN SERIES** **34**

POLTAVA 1709

RUSSIA COMES OF AGE

ANGUS KONSTAM

Russian troops at Poltava, left to right: Fusilier and Praporshchik of the Narvski Regiment, and Line Grenadier of Prince Repnin's Regiment. (Painting by David Rickman)

For a catalogue of
all books published by
Osprey Military,
please write to
The Marketing Manager,
Consumer Catalogue Dept.,
Michelin House, 81 Fulham
Road, London SW3 6RB.

Key to Map Symbols

Army	xxxx ⊠	Brigade	x ⊠	Infantry	⊠
Corps	xxx ⊠	Regiment	III ⊠	Cavalry	◪
Division	xx ⊠	Battalion	II ⊠	Artillery	▫

First published in Great Britain in
1994 by OSPREY, an imprint of Reed
Consumer Books Limited, Michelin
House, 81 Fulham Road, London
SW3 6RB and Auckland, Melbourne
Singapore and Toronto.

ISBN 1-85532-416-4

Produced by DAG Publications Ltd
for Osprey Publishing Ltd.
Colour bird's eye view illustrations by
Cilla Eurich.
Cartography by Micromap.

▶ *Corner of an
entrenched Russian
camp. The firing parapet
is chest high, allowing it
to be manned by both
artillery and infantry
without the need for
embrasures. (Engraving
by Martin the Younger,
early 18th century; State
Historical Museum,
Moscow)*

CONTENTS

THE ORIGINS OF
THE CAMPAIGN

Charles XII of Sweden's invasion of Russia was the first attempt by a major European power to invade the country. The manner in which the campaign was fought, the problems facing the protagonists and its outcome have clear parallels with the invasions of 1812 and 1941. A study of the campaign should therefore provide some degree of insight into the problems facing these later and larger campaigns. It is also of major historic significance, as it brought about the demise of one European power and the rise of another, greater one.

At the start of the campaign in late 1706, Sweden was at the height of her imperial glory. Early seventeenth century campaigns had added Finland, Karelia and Ingria to the Swedish domain, territory that ran around the north coast of the Gulf of Finland. The campaigns of Gustavus Adolphus in Poland and Lithuania had secured the Baltic provinces for Sweden, securing the vital commercial city of Riga. By the end of the Thirty Years War in 1648, Sweden was the possessor of a number of scattered enclaves along the southern coast of the Baltic Sea, which were of great financial benefit to the Swedish state. During the late seventeenth century the political and military aim of the Swedish crown was to maintain this 'imperium'. To achieve this, the country built up an army and navy out of proportion to her size, backed by an impressive military administration.

Under the reigns of Charles X and Charles XI, the empire was maintained – to the great financial benefit of the country; the Baltic Sea was regarded as a Swedish lake, and tariffs ensured that her merchants prospered. However, the Swedish empire was not maintained without incurring the hostility of her neighbours. Denmark, a traditional enemy of Sweden, was concerned about the string of Swedish possessions, such as Bremen and Verden, on her southern border, and sought to renew her long-standing claim to the Duchy of Holstein, a Swedish protectorate. Augustus II, Elector of Saxony, had

also become King of Poland and had inherited Polish claims to their lost territories in Livonia.

In 1689, the young Tsar Peter I wrested control of the Russian state from the regent Sophia. His country was considered an introverted, semi-barbaric state, cut off from the remainder of Europe, which within a few years prompted the young Tsar to adopt a policy of 'westernisation'. It was only a matter of time before he tried to realise his vision of gaining a gateway to the west via the Baltic Sea. As Swedish territory cut the Russian state off from the sea, conflict was inevitable.

When Charles XI died in 1697, he was succeeded to the throne of Sweden by his fifteen-year-old son Charles. This was seen as an opportunity by Sweden's neighbours to dismember the parts of the empire within their own relevant spheres. An alliance was formed between Russia, Denmark and Poland-Saxony, and plans were formed. In April 1700 the Danes invaded Schleswig and Holstein. Two months later the Poles laid siege to Riga. And, later in the season, Tsar Peter led an army into Swedish Livonia and besieged Narva. None of the triumvirate expected the young monarch to be able to retaliate effectively. He was to surprise them all. In late June, he led a Swedish invasion of Zealand, forcing the Danes to sue for peace on 18 August. By October he had shipped a force to Livonia, and on 20 November he defeated a superior Russian army outside Narva. In two short campaigns he had built a reputation as a gifted commander and had restored Sweden's position.

Openly contemptuous of the Russian performance at Narva, Charles did not trouble to follow up his success, which gave them time to recover. Instead, he established a garrison force in Livonia and launched his army on a campaign in Poland, the expressed aim of which was to depose Augustus II. Like Gustavus, Charles XII discovered that he could militarily defeat the Poles whenever he chose,

This Swedish cavalry-man from the Russian campaign carries a French-made flintlock pistol. His tricorn could as easily be replaced by a Karpus. Dragoons were similarly equipped with the obvious addition of a carbine. (Painting by David Rickman)

but that bringing about a favourable and lasting political solution in the country was another thing altogether. For six years his troops marched and countermarched across the length and breadth of Poland, winning victories at Riga (1701), Kliszow (1702), Pulutsk and Thorn (1703), Lemberg and Punitz (1704), Grodno (1705) and Fraustadt (1706). Augustus was deposed and Stanislaus Leszczynski placed on the Polish throne – but he would remain there only with the backing of the Swedish army. In 1705, peace was concluded between Sweden and Poland, which ensured the flow of Polish trade through Swedish Riga and the political and economic isolation of Russia.

Following the Battle of Fraustadt (1706) where an invading Saxon army was comprehensively defeated, Charles XII marched his troops into Saxony, forcing Augüstus to sign the Treaty of Altranstädt, whereby Augustus renounced his claim to the Polish throne and tore up his alliance with Tsar Peter. Charles had knocked two of his three enemies out of the war; he now turned his attention to the third – Russia. While the Swedish army had been marching from victory to victory, Tsar Peter had been conducting several small campaigns around the Gulf of Finland, securing the mouth of the Neva, annexing Ingria and invading Karelia and Livonia. His army was growing in both numbers and experience; but Charles XII and the Swedish army, now at Altranstädt preparing for the forthcoming campaign during the spring and summer of 1707, appeared an unstoppable combination.

◄ *Tsar Peter I (the Great) of Russia (1672–1725). Although he allowed his commanders considerable initiative, he sometimes took direct command of his forces on the battlefield. During the campaign he demonstrated his understanding of the distances and terrain involved in the theatre of operations. (Engraving from The Diary of Peter the Great)*

THE OPPOSING COMMANDERS

Tsar Peter I

Born in 1672, Peter Alexeivitch was introduced to the realities of Muscovite politics at an early age. When he was ten years old his father died and his mother was ousted from power in a military coup orchestrated by the Regent Sophia. Peter was brought up at the summer palace at Preobrazhen-skoi, outside Moscow, spending his time playing at soldiers. His *poteshnye* (play troops) took part in increasingly large mock battles, so by the time of his own accession to power in 1689 – following another coup – he already had the nucleus of a trained and loyal military organisation at his disposal. For the next few years he was content to continue his military training at the hands of foreign advisors, such as Alexander Gordon, a gifted general of Scottish descent.

In 1694–5 he began his first military campaign against the Turkish fortress of Azov, guarding the outlet of the River Don to the Sea of Azov and thus the Black Sea. His *poteshnye* had now become the Russian Guard, and these troops, combined with elements of the older semi-feudal Muscovite army, succeeded in capturing the fortress despite initial setbacks. With his southern border secured, Tsar Peter began to consider his European neighbours.

Throughout his life, Peter displayed a fascination for learning, particularly in the military, maritime and scientific fields. His contacts with western Europe earned him the distrust of many of his orthodox countrymen, but Peter considered the only way forward for Russia was to embrace these occidental methods and reform Russia on a western model. This was reinforced during his travels to Germany, Holland and Britain during 1697–8. Here Peter was introduced to the latest military and naval developments such as new firearm mechanisms and the latest developments in naval architecture. His return to Russia was hastened by a revolt of the Streltsy, the Russian standing army corps, who opposed the reforms he had already put into effect. After brutally crushing the rebellion, the Tsar decided to rebuild the Russian army following the western pattern.

At the outbreak of the Great Northern War in 1700, Russia was only just beginning to change from being a backward-looking semi-feudal state. During the twenty-one years of the conflict Peter continued his policy of reforming the country, while at the same time acting as the head of government, arbiter of diplomatic policy, manager of the economy and supreme head of the armed forces. He displayed an erratic genius for administration and the ability to harness the structure of Russian society and economy to the needs of the state, of which he was the undisputed head. One of his principal social achievements was the conversion of the Russian nobility into instruments of the state, committed to a lifetime of military, diplomatic or civil service.

As a military commander, he was perhaps an intuitive rather than a rational general. His military role was usually that of a 'roving' commander, allowing his generals free reign but retaining the right to step in and take over supreme command when he deemed it necessary. This is reflected in his preference for drafting rules of combat to guide his senior officers rather than demonstrating his tactical wishes by direct example. As a strategist he was perhaps more skilled than Charles XII of Sweden at stepping back from the main field army to determine the role of his other forces, and of using geography to his advantage. His 'scorched earth' policy and the trading of space for time were strategic weapons deployed in the armoury of subsequent Russian strategists, especially in 1812.

His one strategic weakness, his obsession with the protection of his fledgling capital of St. Petersburg, was never exploited by Charles XII.

Following Poltava, Tsar Peter was to mastermind the shift of the war to the offensive and would display an ability to capitalise on the diplomatic kudos resulting from the battle. When the anti-Swedish coalition he created eventually fell apart (through a combination of mistrust of growing Russian power and the attainment of individual national goals), Peter was to continue the war alone, forcing the Swedes to negotiate for peace in 1721. By this, the treaty of Nystadt, Peter would secure the position of Russia as the dominant Baltic power, and her position as a major European player.

His award of the title 'the Great' in 1721 by a grateful Russian senate reflected his considerable achievements. On his death in 1725 his state bore little resemblance to the inward-looking feudal Russia of his childhood; it was a major European power.

Prince Menshikov

Alexander Menshikov (1673–1729) was an early supporter of the young Tsar, and one of the first recruits into the *poteshnye*. As a drinking partner and reformist, he became Peter's closest subject, a position which he used to its full advantage. His military rise resulted from a combination of ability and his close friendship with the Tsar. He participated in the Azov campaign against the Turks and,

◀ *Prince Alexander Danilov Menshikov (1673–1729). Commander of Russian cavalry during the campaign, he displayed considerable ability as an independent commander. He remained the favourite of the Tsar, despite frequent charges of corruption. (The State Hermitage Museum, St. Petersburg)*

▶ *Count Boris Sheremetiev (1652–1719), General Field Marshal and overall commander of the army. His generalship was regarded as solid rather than inspired. During the Battle of Poltava, he took direct control of the Russian infantry. (State Historic Museum, Moscow)*

following the Russia defeat at Narva (1700), he was involved in the reorganisation of the army. He displayed a talent for military command, distinguishing himself during the Ingrian campaign of 1701, notably in the capture of the Noteburg fortress and the clearing of the River Neva. He was trusted with increasingly larger commands, and it was his small army that defeated the Swedes at Kalitz in Poland (1706). During the Swedish invasion of Russia he acted as the overall commander of the Russia cavalry, and it was he who implemented the Russian 'scorched earth' policy.

His performance on the battlefields of Lesnaya and Poltava was adequate rather than inspired; his real ability lay in operational matters and the command of flying columns such as the one that forced the final surrender of the main Swedish army at Perovolochna. During the subsequent campaigns in Poland and Germany he would continue to demonstrate his military capabilities.

During his career Menshikov used his position to secure his power base and to gain financial benefit. His influence is reflected in the Tsar's words: 'He does what he likes without asking my opinion, but I for my part never decide anything without asking him his.' He was continually being accused of corruption, and at times pushed the Tsar's patience to the limit. On Peter's death, Menshikov was to become virtual ruler of Russia, acting as advisor to the Empress Catherine, but on her death he found himself surrounded by enemies. Without the support of a monarch, he was called to account for a lifetime of corruption. He was stripped of his wealth and power and exiled to Siberia where he died within two years.

Count Sheremetiev

Boris Sheremetiev (1652–1719) was a rarity for a late seventeenth century Russian nobleman in that he was travelled and an admirer of occidental ways.

He was therefore a natural supporter of Tsar Peter and his reforms. Before embarking upon a military career he served as a diplomat, representing the Tsar in various European courts. During the Azov campaign (1695–6) he took charge of a diversionary column which captured Turkish fortresses along the lower River Dniepr. At the outbreak of the Swedish war he was given command of the Russian cavalry, a duty he performed with little flair.

He came into his own during the reorganisation of the army, and the Tsar entrusted him with control of the Russia forces facing Livonia. In the subsequent Livonian campaign (1702) he produced the first victories for Peter, at Erestfer and Hummelshof, for which he was promoted Field Marshal. When the Swedish invasion came, Sheremetiev was given overall command of the Russia foot, while on occasion being awarded independent command. He was entrusted with the army while it shadowed Charles XII during the march into the Ukraine. At Poltava he reverted to his normal role as commander of the foot.

For the last decade of his life he was to concern himself with conducting military reforms before retiring to his estates. As a commander he was considered cautious – dependable rather than brilliant – and as such provided a perfect counter-balance to Menshikov and the Tsar.

King Charles XII

The military enigma of his age, Charles was born in 1682, the only surviving male heir of Charles XI and Queen Eleonora. From an early age he was fascinated by military history, and in later years is reputed to have carried a biography of Alexander the Great with him on campaign. At his coronation in 1697, monarchs of the countries surrounding the Swedish empire saw their opportunity: they could not see how this youth would be able to maintain Swedish power. He was 18 when the Great Northern War broke out, and within a year had forced the Danes to sign a humiliating peace treaty and defeated Peter's fledgling Russian army at Narva. The leaders of the European powers were forced to revise their opinion of Charles and his exploits were eagerly followed and enhanced by contemporary writers; Voltaire called him the young warrior king.

▲ *King Charles XII of Sweden (1682–1718). The charismatic 'warrior-king', he spent half his life campaigning in defence of his Swedish possessions. His injury prior to the Battle of Poltava meant that once battle was joined he became little more than a bystander, when his active involvement might have changed the outcome of events. (Royal Armouries)*

He has been described as proud, courageous and strong-headed. He has also been called rash and obstinate. His victories gained him an aura of invincibility, a feeling shared both by the king and his men. This, backed by an experienced army, proved an unstoppable combination during what was to become a whirlwind military career, with a string of victories over the Saxon-Polish army during the period 1702–6. This was a time when Charles encountered both political frustrations and military glory.

His reputation was based on a sound rapport with his soldiers, and on the battlefield this enabled him to conduct attacks that for other generals of the period would have been considered foolhardy. At the operational level, he was quick to grasp that in the East the campaigning season could be extended into the winter, when the hard ground and frozen rivers helped rather than hindered the movement of troops.

In Poland he fought a campaign to impose a political solution through military means. It can be argued that he regarded politics as a device to be employed after the final battle was won; in this Tsar Peter employed a more practical approach, using both war and diplomacy to achieve his ends.

Charles was a Lutheran, and devoutly religious. As with his subjects, this resulted in a deep fatalism, which was a strength when all was going well. It was also a weakness that accounted for the collapse of his military machine when it was defeated.

His leg wound on the eve of Poltava possibly denied the Swedes the chance of victory. The absense of his direct control of the army exposed the rivalry between Rehnskold and Lewenhaupt with catastrophic results.

Count Rehnskold

Carl Gustav Rehnskold (1651–1722) was one of Charles XII's most able lieutenants, a vital element in the King's military legend. He was a skilful and experienced soldier, becoming a colonel at 26 and serving both Charles and his father with distinction. The Swedish General Stenbock said of the Battle of Narva: 'It is God's work alone, but if there is anything human in it, it is the firm, immovable resolution of his Majesty and the ripe dispositions of General Rehnskold.'

His greatest military triumph was his victory over the Saxons and Russians at Fraustadt (1706), where he annihilated a far more numerous enemy

▲ *Field Marshal Carl Gustav Rehnskold (1652–1722). Field Marshal of the Swedish army and Charles XII's senior commander. Because of the incapacitation of the King, he took direct control of the Swedish army prior to the Battle of Poltava. (Swedish National Portrait Gallery, Stockholm)*

army. Fraustadt also brought him a reputation for ruthlessness, when he sanctioned the massacre of Russian prisoners after the battle. Already Charles's General of Cavalry, he was promoted field marshal for his efforts. During the invasion of Russia he led

◄ Count Adam Ludwig Lewenhaupt (1659–1719). General of Infantry, he commanded the Swedish supply column decimated at the Battle of Lesnaya. *At Poltava he took control of the Swedish infantry, and led their final charge. (Swedish National Portrait Gallery, Stockholm)*

His subordinates described him as haughty and rude, and his strong dislike for General Lewenhaupt was to cause a fatal rift in the command structure on the day of battle.

Count Lewenhaupt

Adam Ludwig Lewenhaupt (*Leijonhufvud* in Swedish) (1659–1719) was a well educated, religious aristocrat, whose first choice was the diplomatic corps rather than the army. Finding no career opportunities, however, he entered military service abroad, fighting in Bavarian and Dutch service before joining the Swedish army on the eve of the Great Northern War. Given independent command, he proved himself a reliable but uninspired commander. By 1706 he had risen to the rank of General of Infantry, and was also the Governor of Riga, holding Swedish Livonia for the King.

As a commander, he was considered cautious and considerate of the welfare of his men. His handling of the supply column during the Russian invasion has been seen as lethargic, the delay in reaching the King's army being blamed for the subsequent disasters. This is an unfair assessment given the logistical problems he faced. At Poltava he was suffering from diarrhoea, which probably accounted for his poor performance. A further hindrance to the Swedish cause was the personality clash between Lewenhaupt and Rehnskold.

He was to command the Swedish army during the retreat following Poltava, and his decision to surrender the remains of the army at Perovolochna, avoiding needless bloodshed demonstrated his concern for his troops. He died a prisoner in Moscow.

the cavalry at Holowczyn, was wounded during the assault on Veprik and took direct control over the army when the King was wounded before Poltava. Although following the plans drawn up by Charles, it was Rehnskold who carried the responsibility of overall command at Poltava.

THE OPPOSING ARMIES

The Swedish Army

The army inherited by Charles from his father Charles XI (1660–97) was one imbued with an already illustrious reputation and a set of distinctive military doctrines.

The period from Gustavus Adolphus until Poltava represented the pinnacle of Sweden's position as a major European political and military power, a status maintained by her small but professional army. Under Charles XII the Swedes were widely regarded as being the best and most aggressive soldiers in Europe. Contemporaries said of them that they were never concerned with the number of their enemy, only where they were. This spirit was supported by a fatalistic Lutheran belief, which saw death as unavoidable when the Lord chose, creating an almost rash attitude towards danger. Such strengths could also be fatally exploited, as happened during the campaign in Russia.

The Infantry

Sweden in the 1700s had meagre resources of finance and manpower to maintain her Baltic empire. In order to maintain an army commensurate with her status, Sweden employed the *Indelningsverk* (allotment method). This system made collections of farms responsible for providing a fully equipped soldier. In peacetime, these men worked the land in their supporting area, and in times of war it allowed an army of 40,000 men to be put into the field at negligible cost to the state. Further men

▶ *Swedish line Infantryman, c. 1700–12. The model wears the knee-length coat introduced by Charles XI, with its distinctive waist pleats. The cuffs were smaller than* *those in contemporary use in other armies. The model also carries a sword, cartridge box and flintlock musket. (National Army Museum, Stockholm)*

▲ Swedish Pikeman, c. 1700–12. This figure displays the Swedish coat clearly; also the habit of wearing overstockings on campaign. The unusual headgear is a karpus; a lined woollen hat with a large brim that could be turned back to expose the lining. (Drawing by S. Hart. First reproduced in Eighteenth Century Notes and Queries, published by Partisan Press, UK)

▲ Swedish Dragoon, c. 1700–12. In general, the Swedish cavalry were clothed and equipped as the infantry. Karpuses were also issued to mounted units. Although Swedish dragoons were issued with carbines, in battle they were employed as shock troops like any other form of Swedish horse. (Drawing by S. Hart. First reproduced in Eighteenth Century Notes and Queries, published by Partisan Press, UK)

could be raised from the same area if extra manpower were requested.

When called up, 50 such men mustered in a local centre, forming a *Korporalskap*, three of which then being grouped into a *Kompani*. These then gathered at a provincial centre to form a *Battaljon* of 4 *Kompanis*, or 600 men in total. Each province supplied one or two regiments, each consisting of two such battalions. This meant that these units retained a strongly territorial nature. This system was also adopted in the Swedish provinces of Finland and Livonia. In addition, a handful of regiments were organised as a full-time standing army. These *varvarde* units included the Swedish guard regiments and were raised using direct state revenue.

One third of each battalion were issued with pikes, an anachronism in contemporary Europe but a practice also employed by the Russians. Musketeers carried modern flintlock muskets, and all infantrymen were equipped with swords.

On the battlefield a battalion would form in four ranks, with the pikemen grouped in the centre. Alternatively, the pikes were grouped in the centre of each company, giving four pike stands per battalion. The two equal wings of musketeers would each be flanked by grenadiers. Unlike other European armies, there is no evidence that these grenadiers were grouped into *ad hoc* grenadier battalions, except in the Foot Guard Regiment, where the grenadiers formed an extra battalion. (This regiment had three battalions in addition to the grenadiers).

The standard Carolean tactic was to fire a volley from the front two ranks at 50 paces; then on the order, 'Gå på' (fall on) they would charge the enemy with bayonets fixed and pikes levelled. Against unsteady troops this doctrine proved highly successful. It was only at Poltava that the rashness of the tactic was exposed; launched in insufficient strength against a prepared enemy.

The Cavalry

The *Indelningsverk* system was similarly applied to the raising of cavalry and dragoon regiments. Individual local yeomen farmers committed themselves to providing a trooper in return for exemption from conscription and some forms of taxation. The farm

▲ *Swedish artilleryman, c. 1700–21. Artillery wore the same type of coat as other arms, but did not turn back the skirt. Unlike the rest of the army, they wore mid-grey coats and carried a small-sword for personal protection. The figure is depicted holding a Swedish linstock, signifying his position as gun captain. (Drawing by S. Hart. First reproduced in Eighteenth Century Notes and Queries, published by Partisan Press, UK)*

Swedish Order of Battle at Holowczyn, 3 July 1708

Initial Assault Forces (Charles XII)

Life Guard Regiment
  (4 battalions)
Dalcarian Regiment
  (2 battalions)

General Bunow's Artillery

Eighteen 6 pounders
Eight 12 pounders
Two Howitzers

A force of 600 Valaks accompanied the King but remained on the western bank of the stream, around the village of Novoe Selo.

REINFORCEMENTS ABOUT 2.40 A.M.
Maj. Gen. Sparre's Command
Ostgotland Regiment
  (2 battalions)

Uppland Regiment
  (2 battalions)
Vastmanland Regiment
  (2 battalions)

REINFORCEMENTS ABOUT 3.00 A.M.
Maj. Gen. Creutz's Command
Life Guard Cavalry Regiment
Drabanten Guard
  (squadron strength)
Life Guard Dragoon Regiment
Nyland Cavalry Regiment
Smaland Cavalry regiment
Ostgotland Cavalry Regiment

Creutz was accompanied by Field Marshal Rehnskold.

---

was then termed a *Rusthall* and became the local mustering and training centre.

Normal regimental strength was around 500 men, divided into two squadrons, each of two troops (or companies in the case of dragoons). On campaign, full-strength companies were sometimes also referred to as squadrons. Prior to the Russian campaign, regimental strength averaged 1,060 men, more than double the normal complement. This demonstrates a certain flexibility which allowed for the absorption of German recruits, as well as the acceptance that attrition rates would be high during the campaign. *Varvarde* regiments were also usually larger than normal formations. Mounted troops accounted for an exceptionally high percentage of the whole army – almost 50%, compared with the contemporary European norm of about 25%.

The Swedish cavalry demonstrated the same offensive mentality as the infantry. Squadrons in the field would be drawn up in a line three ranks deep, bent into a chevron shape (or linear wedge). Troopers were directed to ride knee behind knee, forming a cohesive unit that was difficult to break up. Charges were launched at about 150 paces from the enemy line and pressed home using the sword at the point (i.e., for thrusting rather than for cutting). Officers and cornets appear to have formed the apex of the wedge to encourage momentum and cohesion. The practice of firing from the saddle was not employed, as was the case in a number of European armies, including that of Russia. Dragoons retained the ability to fight dismounted, as during the assault on Veprik.

The Artillery

Charles XII entered Russia with a small but modern field artillery train consisting of light and medium guns. This was organised into an artillery regiment for administrative purposes, with base depots in

---

Swedish Order of Battle at Lesnaya, 28 September 1708

Commander: General Sheremetiev

INFANTRY

Col. Meierfeld's Brigade
Abo Regiment (1 battalion)
Oesterbotten Regiment
  (1 battalion)
Helsinge Regiment
  (1 battalion)
Oeselholm Regiment
  (1 battalion)
Smaland Tremmenings Regiment (1 battalion)

Col. Stackelberg's Brigade
Bjoerneborg Regiment
  (2 battalions)
Nyland Regiment
  (1 battalion)
Abo & Bjoerneborg Tremmenings Regiment (1 battalion)
Uppland Tremmenings Regiment (1 battalion)

CAVALRY
Col. Armfeldt's Brigade
Abo & Bjoernborg Cavalry Regiment

Karelian Cavalry Regiment
Adelsfahn Cavalry Regiment

ARTILLERY
Eleven 4-pdr regimental guns (allocated to the battalions)
Six 6-pdr field guns in a large single battery

REINFORCEMENTS (arrived during the battle after being recalled from Propoitsk)

Brig. Gen. Schlitterfeldt's Brigade
Karelian Dragoon Regiment
Schlitterfeldt's Livonian Dragoon Regiment
Skoge's Livonian Dragoon Battalion

Col. Wennerstedt's Brigade
Upplands Standsdragon Regiment
Schlippenbach's Livonian Dragoon Regiment
Oesel Dragoon Battalion

Swedish Order of Battle, Poltava, 28 June 1709

Commander in Chief: Charles XII (escorted by 24 foot guards and 12 Drabants)
Commander in the field: Field Marshal Rehnskold (also commander of cavalry)

START OF THE BATTLE

LEFT FLANK CAVALRY (Maj. Gen. Hamilton)
First Column (Prince of Wuremburg) (1,650 men)
Ostgotland Cavalry Regiment
Abo Cavalry Regiment
Skanska Cavalry Regiment
Second Column (Col. Torstensson) (1,050 men)
Uppland Tremanning Cavalry Regiment
Nyland Cavalry Regiment
Third Column (Col. Gyllensterna) (1,100 men)
Ducker's Dragoon Regiment
Gyllensterna Dragoon Regiment

RIGHT FLANK CAVALRY (Maj. Gen. Creutz)
Fourth Column (Col. Heilm) (1,350 men)
Sodra Skanska Cavalry Regiment (1/2 sized)
Taube's Dragoon Regiment
Hielm's Dragoon Regiment

Fifth Column (Col. Horn) (1,000 men)
Smalands Cavalry Regiment
Norra Skanska Cavalry Regiment
Sixth Column (Col. Hard) (1,650 men)
Life Dragoon Regiment
Life Drabants (1 squadron)
Life Cavalry regiment (12 instead of 8 troops)

INFANTRY COLUMNS (General Lewenhaupt)
First Column (Maj. Gen. Sparre) (2,600 men)
Vastmanland Regiment (2 battalions)
Narke Varmlands Regiment (2 battalions)
Jonkopings Regiment (1 battalion)
Second Column (Maj. Gen. Stackelberg) (1,670 men)
Vasterbotten Regiment (2 battalions)
Ostgotland Regiment (1 battalion)
Uppland Regiment (2 battalions)
Third Column (Maj. Gen. Roos) (2,000 men)
Dalcarian Regiment (2 battalions)
Foot Guard Regiment (2nd and 3rd battalions)
Fourth column (Maj. Gen. Lagercrona) (1,400 men)
Foot Guards Regiment (1st and Gren. battalions)

Kalmar Regiment (1 battalion)
Skaraborg Regiment (1 battalion)

Artillery (Capt. Clerckberg)
Four 4 pounder regimental guns

INFANTRY LINE AT THE FINAL STAGE
Battalions are listed from right to left
Commander: General Lewenhaupt

1st Bn Life Guard Regiment (Capt. Gadde)
Grenadier Bttn. Life Guard Regiment (Capt. Rosentierna)
Skaraborg Regiment (Col. Ulfsparre)
Kalmar Regiment (Col. Ranck)
2nd Bn Life Guard Regiment (Capt. Mannersvard)
2nd Bn Uppland Regiment (Lt Col von Post)
1st Bn Uppland Regiment (Col Stiernhook)
Ostgota Regiment (Col Appelgren)
2nd Bn Narke-Varmland Regiment (Col Wrangel)

To their rear and left:
1st Bn Vastmanland Regiment (Maj Reuter)
2nd Bn Vastmanland Regiment (Lt Col Wrangel)

Riga, Göteborg and Stockholm. The main calibres employed were 6-pounders and 12-pounders for the field artillery, supported by 4-pounder regimental guns.

In practice, the transport difficulties encountered in Poland and Russia meant that all but the regimental guns had difficulty keeping up with the main army. It has been said that Charles XII was contemptuous of his artillery arm, although he used it to good effect at Holowczyn. It is probably more accurate to say that the nature of his aggressive battlefield tactics meant that the artillery was of only limited value once battle was joined.

The Russian Army

When Tsar Peter I came to power in 1689 he inherited a Russian army that was essentially semi-feudal.

His childhood had been spent playing live wargames with his *poteshnye* (play troops) organised on occidental lines. Following the experiences of his first campaign against the Turks, he decided to raise a new army based on the western model. This force, formed in 1700, was launched into the Great Northern War with no experience and little training against some of the most professional troops in Europe. Peter was fortunate that, following their almost inevitable defeat at Narva, the army was allowed to recover and reorganise without interference by Charles XII. The Swedish king regarded the Russians as unworthy opponents, turning his back on them to campaign in Poland. This six-year respite was used to conduct limited campaigns in Livonia and around St. Petersburg, allowing the army to build up its confidence and experience. When Charles began his Russian campaign he was

▲ *Russian musketeer c. 1708–9. He wears the pre-1720 pattern Russian army coat and waistcoat and is depicted loading a Dutch-made flintlock musket of the kind bought in large numbers by Rus-sia immediately prior to the campaign. (Drawing by S. Hart. First repro-duced in Eighteenth Century Notes and Queries, published by Partisan Press, UK)*

▲ *Russian pikeman c. 1708–9. Unlike the Swedes, only one infantrymen in four was a pikeman. Anachronistic by contemporary occiden-tal standards, they were retained as a means of offsetting the superior offensive quality of Swedish cavalry. (Draw-ing by S. Hart. First reproduced in Eighteenth Century Notes and Queries, published by Partisan Press, UK)*

▶ *Russian line infantry fusiliers, c. 1700–20. Two of the figures are wearing the kartuz, an alternative form of headgear adopted by many Russian regiments. Note the variety of longarms depicted, representative of the haphazard manner in which Peter's army was equipped. (Engraving from Viskovatov's Rossiskoi Imperatorski Armii, St. Petersburg, 1844–56)*

to encounter an army markedly different from the one he met at Narva.

The Infantry

Peter's *poteshnye* were converted into two guard regiments in 1698, and the new foot regiments were organised and equipped using them as a model. The organisation of these underwent a number of changes, but by the start of the Swedish invasion each battalion consisted of four companies, each of about 150 men. A regiment (*polk*) was formed from two (or occasionally three) battalions, supported by a battery of two 3-pounder regimental guns. In theory each regiment also had a grenadier company attached, but these were almost all concentrated into grenadier battalions. In 1708 the grenadiers were permanently grouped into grenadier regiments, each of two battalions. Exceptions to regimental sizes were the Preobrazhenski and Semenovski guard regiments, which boasted four and three battalions respectively, and enlarged batteries of regimental artillery. Both

Peter the Great at Poltava, with a Grenadier of the Preobrazhenski Regiment. The Tsar's uniform is based on that preserved in the State Historical Museum. (Painting by David Rickman)

Russian Order of Battle at Holowczyn, 3 July 1708

Overall commander: None

MAJOR GENERAL REPNIN'S DIVISION
(listed as deployed, from north to south)

Brig. Gen. Schweden's Brigade
Repnin's Grenadier regiment (2 battalions)
Ryazanski Regiment (2 battalions)
Lefort's Regiment (2 battalions)
Rostovski Regiment (2 battalions)

Brig. Gen. Chamber's Brigade
Vyatski Regiment (2 battalions)
Narvski Regiment (3 battalions)
Tobolski Regiment (2 battalions)
Koporski Regiment (2 battalions)

Attached artillery
Eight 8 pounders
Four Howitzers

REINFORCEMENTS

Maj. Gen Goltz's Division
(arriving from south)

Brig. Gen. Ilfland's Brigade
Pskovski Dragoon Regiment
Tverski Dragoon Regiment

Brig. Gen. Heinsk's Brigade
Tobolski Dragoon Regiment
Byeloserski Dragoon Regiment
Vladmirski Dragoon Regiment

Prince of Hesse Darmstadt's Brigade
Viatski Dragoon Regiment
Smolenski Dragoon Regiment
Rostovski Dragoon Regiment

Maj. Gen. Renne's Command
(arriving from north)
Astrakhanski Regiment (2 battalions)
Pskovski Regiment (2 battalions)
Ingermanlandski Regiment (2 battalions)

(These troops were detached from Sheremetiev's Division).

---

of these regiments also retained their grenadier companies, and the Preobrazhenski Regiment also boasted a unit of bombardiers equipped with hand mortars.

Up to 1 in 5 infantrymen were armed with pikes, thus imitating their Swedish counterparts. By the time of the Poltava campaign the fusiliers were armed with modern flintlock muskets, and all soldiers carried swords.

Tactical doctrine favoured the use of firepower to counter the Swedish *gå på* approach, and field fortifications were favoured to hinder any frontal attack. Battalions formed up in four ranks, with the pikemen grouped in the centre. Firing was based upon the Prussian or Anglo-Dutch model, the troops being trained to fire either by ranks or by platoons. The production of a set of rules of combat in 1708, based upon the experiences of the war so far, meant that tactics were adapted to most effectively counter the Swedish *modus operandi*.

The Cavalry

In 1700 there were only two regular cavalry regiments in the army, but by the time of the Swedish invasion this had been expanded to 34 regiments, all of dragoons. Peter favoured this troop type over heavier cavalry as they were more able to adapt to the operational roles he demanded of his horse:

Russian Order of Battle, Lesnaya, 28 September 1708

Commander: Tsar Peter I

TSAR PETER I'S DIVISION

Maj. Gen Golovin's Command
Preobrazhenski Guard Regiment (3 battalions)
Seminovski Guard Regiment (3 battalions)
Astrakhanski Regiment (1 battalion)

Col. Roshnev's Brigade
Troitski Dragoon Regiment
Tverski Dragoon Regiment
Nischegorodski Dragoon Regiment

PRINCE MENSHIKOV'S DIVISION:

Col. Verden's Brigade
Ingermanlandski Regiment (3 battalions)

Col. Meshtierski's Brigade
Vladmirski Dragoon Regiment
Sibirski Dragoon Regiment
Smolenski Dragoon Regiment

Col. Campbell's Brigade
Nevski Dragoon Regiment
Rostovski Dragoon Regiment
Viatski Dragoon Regiment

Artillery
Eight 2 pounder horse artillery guns accompanied the Russian flying column.

REINFORCEMENTS – MAJ GEN BAUER'S DIVISION:

Brig. Gen. Behm's Brigade
Koporski Dragoon Regiment
Yambourgski Dragoon Regiment
Permski Dragoon Regiment
Kargopolski Dragoon Regiment

Brig. Gen. Shaumburg's Brigade
Kievski Dragoon Regiment
Narvski Dragoon Regiment
Ustiugski Dragoon Regiment
Novgorodski Dragoon Regiment

◀ *Russian dragoon trooper, c. 1700–20. He is equipped with an unusual shortened musket with a serpentine trigger. The Tsar regarded dragoons as the most useful form of regular cavalry, given the particular nature of the eastern European theatre. (Engraving from Viskovatov's Rossiskoi Imperatorski Armii, St. Petersburg, 1844–56)*

scouting, screening, ravaging and raiding, as well as being employed on the battlefield.

Dragoon regiments consisted of ten companies, each of about 100 men, which could be paired up to form five squadrons. A reform of some regiments produced twelve company regiments operating in four squadrons but this was only partly implemented by the start of the campaign. In theory each regiment would also include a horse grenadier company, but these were removed (in 1708) to form three new horse grenadier regiments. These operated in a manner similar to normal dragoon regiments. In addition, two conventional cavalry squadrons existed; the escorts of Prince Menshikov and Count Sheremetiev.

Russian dragoon regiments deployed in three ranks, each with a frontage of four or five companies.

►*Don Cossack , early 18th century. The figure is depicted wearing the traditional elements of Cossack costume: kaftan, baggy trousers and boots. Both sides employed Cossacks as scouts, raiders and harriers. (Engraving from Viskovatov's Rossiskoi Imperatorski Armii, St. Petersburg, 1844–56)*

Russian Order of Battle, Poltava, 28 June 1709, Final Stage

Commander in Chief: Tsar Peter I
Chief of Staff: Maj Gen Werden

LEFT FLANK CAVALRY (Menshikov)
He directly commanded the division.
Escort: Prince Menshikov's Life
Squadron

Col. Radetski's Brigade
Life Dragoon Regiment
Kievski Dragoon Regiment
Ingermanlandski Dragoon Regiment

Col. Volkonski's Brigade
Vologodski Dragoon Regiment
Novgorodski Dragoon Regiment
Yaroslavski Dragoon Regiment

INFANTRY LINE (Field Marshal Sheremetiev)

MAJ GEN HALLART'S DIVISION
Col Lignitz's Brigade
Busch's Grenadier Regiment
    (2 battalions)
Nischerovgorodski Regiment
    (2 battalions)
Col Pfennigbeir's Brigade
Kazanski Regiment (2 battalions)
Pskovski Regiment (2 battalions)
Col Tiernischev's Brigade
Sibirski Regiment (2 battalions)
Moskovski Regiment (3 battalions)

MAJ GEN REPNIN'S DIVISION
Col Sasiekin's Brigade
Butyrski Regiment (2 battalions)
Novgorodski Regiment (2 battalions)
Lt Col Sukin's Brigade
Narvski Regiment (3 battalions)
Schlusselburgski Regiment
    (2 battalions)
Col Leslie's Brigade
Kievski Regiment (3 battalions)
Repnin's Grenadier Regiment
    (2 battalions)

MAJ GEN GOLITSIN'S DIVISION
Maj Gen Van Belling's Brigade
Astrakhanski Regiment (2 battalions)
Ingermanlandski Regiment
    (3 battalions)
Lt Col Kuriakin's Brigade

Semenovski Guard Regiment (3 battalions)
Lt. Col. Dolgoruki's Brigade
Preobrazhenski Guard Regiment (4 battalions)
Bieltz's Grenadier Regiment (1 battalion)

The infantry were deployed in two ranks, each regiment having one battalion in each line (two in the first line in the case of the three battalion regiments). The Preobrazhenski Regiment had two in each line, and Birltz's Grenadier Regiment had its sole battalion in the first line. The lines therefore consisted of: First Line, 24 battalions; reserve Line, 18 battalions. Regimental guns were all deployed in the spaces between battalions in the first line (77 guns in all).

RIGHT FLANK CAVALRY (Bauer)

MAJ. GEN. BEHM'S DIVISION:
Col. Kropotov's Brigade
Kropotov Horse Grenadier Regiment
Archangelski Dragoon Regiment
Nevski Dragoon Regiment
Col. Tiernischov's Brigade
Byeloserski Dragoon Regiment
Vyatski Dragoon Regiment
Nischenovgorodski Dragoon Regiment

MAJ. GEN. SCHAUMBURG'S DIVISION
Col. Meschtierski's Brigade
Sibirski Dragoon Regiment
Vladmirski Dragoon Regiment
Moskovski Dragoon Regiment
Col. Van der Roop's Brigade
Van der Roop Horse Grenadier Regiment
Roshnev's Horse Grenadier Regiment
The General's Dragoon Company

Note: Bauer's cavalry deployed in two lines. Each regiment had two squadrons forward and two back.

NORTHERN CAVALRY (Hetman Skoropadski)
An unknown number of Cossacks.
Estimated at about 1,500

CAMP GARRISON (Col. Gunther)
Col. Abraham's Brigade
Bieltz's Grenadier Regiment (1 Battalion)
Apraxin's Regiment (1 Battalion)
Troitski Regiment (2 Battalions)
Col. Munsterman's Brigade
von Rentzel's Regiment (2 Battalions)
Lefortski Regiment (2 Battalions)
du Bois' Grenadier Regiment (1 Battalion)

RENTZEL'S FORCE (Maj. Gen. Rentzel)

MAJ. GEN. HEINSKE'S DIVISION
Col. Roshnev's Brigade
Tverski Dragoon Regiment
Riazanski Dragoon Regiment
Permski Dragoon Regiment
Col. Meschtierski's Brigade
Novotroitski Dragoon Regiment
Narvski Dragoon Regiment
Azovski Dragoon Regiment
Col. von Fichtenheim's Brigade
Fischtenheim Regiment (1 Battalion)
Tobolski Regiment (2 Battalions)
Koporski Regiment (2 Battalions)
Col. Golovin's Brigade
Rostovski Regiment (2 Battalions)
du Bois' Grenadier Regiment (1 Battalion)

Note: Golovin's Brigade were dispatched from the fortified camp about 9:00 am, when Roos barricaded his men inside the abandoned redoubt.

REDOUBT GARRISONS (Colonel Augustov)
Byelgorodski Regiment (2 Battalions)
One battalion held redoubt 3, the remaining battalion was divided between the other 10 redoubts.

They were trained to discharge their firearms (carbines or shortened muskets) when approximately 30 paces from the enemy, then to advance to contact at the trot, with swords drawn. Lacking the training of their Swedish counterparts, advancing at the trot and putting emphasis on firepower was the only way the cohesion of the unit could be maintained. Against cavalry it was hoped that the volley would disrupt the enemy enough to allow the Russians to fight on more equal terms once the units clashed. As an experiment, Peter also employed a number of horse artillery batteries to enhance cavalry firepower, but these were disbanded after the Poltava campaign.

The Cossacks

A quasi-military caste, the Cossack communities of the Ukraine, the lower Dniepr (the Zaporozhne) and the Don all participated in the campaign, the first two as allies of the Swedes. (In other words Cossacks fought on both sides during the campaign.) The Swedes also employed a number of Polish Valaks, Cossacks from Polish lands who served the state as auxiliary troops.

The host was divided into regiments based on territorial roots, which in turn were composed of company sized *sotnias* (hundreds). These were subdivided into *kurens* (troops) of up to fifty riders.

They operated as scouts and raiders for both armies, and the Russians in particular made extensive use of them to harry the enemy. Jefferyes wrote that they 'use all the methods of the most experienc'd soldiers to allarm us, and keep us for the most part both day and night, with one foot in the stirrup'.

However, these light horsemen were of little use on the battlefield, and in all the major engagements of the campaign did little but sit on the sidelines, awaiting the opportunity to pursue the enemy once beaten. The exception were the Zaporozhne, whom Charles employed as infantry in the Poltava siege lines. Standard Cossack weapons included sabres, pistols, muskets, rifled hunting muskets and lightweight lances.

The Artillery Train

The Russian use of regimental artillery and horse batteries has already been mentioned. In addition, the Tsar's army boasted a large and well maintained train of medium and heavy artillery and mortars. For administrative purposes this was organised into an artillery regiment divided into companies. Apart from 2- and 3-pounders (used for horse and regimental batteries respectively), the principal calibre employed was an 8-pounder piece, although at times 12-pounders, howitzers and mortars were also used in the field.

Peter employed these to great effect; regimental guns were used to supplement infantry firepower, while the main battery pieces used in a more conventional role were deployed to devastating effect at Poltava. The Tsar was certainly Charles's superior in ability to understand the potential of artillery on the battlefield.

▼ *Russian military musket, c.1709. The weapon is a 'fusil', fitted with a doglock hammer mechanism, which was common on the majority of longarms in Peter's army. No regulation pattern existed and much of the army was* *equipped with imported weapons, the average bore size being about 16mm. (Line drawing by the author from an original in the collection of the State Historical Museum, Moscow)*

THE OPPOSING PLANS

When King Charles XII drew up plans for his proposed invasion of Russia he had the best of material to work from: Gyllenkrok, his Quartermaster General had purchased large numbers of maps of Poland and Russia, which included a detailed map of Russia presented by Augustus II. Unlike his earlier campaigns, there is no direct evidence of Charles XII's intended plan of operation since all army papers

◀ *Quartermaster General Axel Gyllenkrok (1655–1730). He was Charles XII's principal operational planner, whose collection of route maps and reports were used by the King to prepare for the campaign. According to historian R. M. Hatton, he was an acknowledged 'expert on roads'. Gyllenkrok was also given the task of drawing up the final order of battle for the Swedish army at Poltava. (Royal Armouries)*

were destroyed at Perovolochna, after Poltava. Despite this, certain aspects can be pieced together. Suggestions that either he had no plan or that he intended to move south anyway can be discounted.

His main war aims were to free the occupied areas of his Baltic empire, and to achieve a lasting peace that would allow him to return to the main European stage. The former would in preference be achieved without letting the Baltic States become a battleground.

For the first stage, he hoped to manoeuvre the Russians out of Poland as quickly as possible to avoid further devastation to a country that was now allied to the Swedish cause through a puppet king. The move through the Masurian Forest conducted in January 1708 was an outflanking operation planned long in advance.

Once on the border of Russia, the options were to head north towards St. Petersburg, forward to Moscow or south into the Ukraine, and then on to Moscow with Turkish help. The former risked Swedish Livonia becoming a battleground, while the lack of preparatory diplomatic negotiations with both Cossacks and Turks indicates that movement

►*Count Carl Piper, First Minister of Sweden (1647–1716). The only cabinet member to accompany the King on campaign, he was charged with organising the diplomatic element of the operation. Captured at Poltava, he was regarded as the senior Swedish prisoner after the battle. (Royal Armouries)*

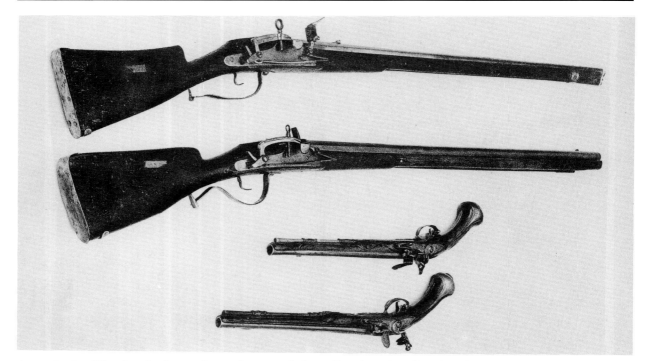

through the Ukraine had not formed part of the original plan. The plan of campaign was thus an advance on Moscow along the only direct route open to Charles – through Smolensk (the general route taken by Napoleon in 1812).

The circulating of pre-printed propaganda leaflets around Smolensk prior to the Swedish approach underlines the fact that this was the intended route. Movement through the 'river gate' (the gap between the Rivers Dvina and Dniepr) would negate the long north-south river barrier that was encountered on all other parts of the Russian border. When the army did march, Charles headed straight for this area.

Once in the Russian capital, terms could be forced on the Tsar. Writing in 1713, Charles discounted any claims that he planned to depose the Tsar as he had Augustus of Poland, stressing the difference between a 'natural' monarch and a mere 'elected' one, as Augustus was.

On the Russian part, the main weapons were space, terrain and weather. It was hoped that Menshikov's army in Poland would be able to delay the Swedish advance long enough for the Tsar to organise the defence of the Russian borders. It was never intended to hold Poland. If the Russians laid it to waste this would so fatigue the pursuing Swedes that by the time they reached the main Russian army they would be at a distinct disadvantage. If the war were carried as far as the Russian border, then Peter was quite prepared to continue the scorched-earth policy as far as Moscow. The comment attributed to the Countess Sieniawksa – that it was a policy comparable to a husband cutting off his balls to spite his wife – may well have been apposite!

The main directive visible in the Tsar's letters was the need to defend St. Petersburg at all costs. This was his Achilles' heel, and a deeper understanding of Peter's obsession with his city would have been of great benefit to the Swedish king. During the Swedish march through the 'river gates' the deployment of the bulk of his army between the Swedes and St. Petersburg was indicative of this obsession. Charles ordered General Lübecker, his commander in Finland, to demonstrate against Peter's capital, but there was no intention other than to tie down Russian troops that might be needed elsewhere. If the Swedish plan had instead been a reinforced drive from Finland, coordinated with a force combining the main Swedish army under the King and General Lewenhaupt's Livonian army, then the outcome of the campaign might have been radically different.

THE CAMPAIGN

Through Poland

On 27 August 1707, Charles XII of Sweden rode out of Altranstadt in Saxony at the head of his army. By 7 September his troops were crossing the Oder at Steinau, which at that time marked the Polish border. Prince Menshikov's Russian army in Poland fell back to the east, abandoning western Poland to the Swedes. On the Tsar's orders he instituted a scorched-earth policy, burning crops and buildings, killing or driving off livestock and poisoning wells. Poland had once again become the battleground between two great powers.

◀ *Swedish firearms, c.1709. Both longarms are examples of those issued to the Swedish army, and are of Swedish manufacture. Although 'baltic-lock' flintlock pieces, they retain characteristics common to earlier weapons. Of the two pistols, the longer is for use by cavalry, while the smaller example would probably have been used by an officer. All of these weapons were reputedly captured at Poltava. (State Historical Museum, Moscow)*

Poland and Eastern Russia, 1708–9

▲ *Although not painted in eastern Europe, this depiction of a French encampment during the Marlburian campaigns reflects the standard contemporary appearance of camp life. Note the tented horse stalls in regimented lines, with tents for soldiers and officers behind them. (By an unknown artist, early eighteenth century, Royal Armouries)*

during the last days of 1707 the Swedes crossed the now frozen river. Menshikov withdrew. Rather than follow in the wasteland left by the Russians, Charles led his army through Masovia (Masuria), a region of forest and swamp adjacent to East Prussia (a move similar to the German advance through the Ardennes in 1940, bypassing prepared lines of defence by a march through seemingly impassable terrain).

A hard-fought guerrilla war erupted between the Swedish army and the local peasants, who resented the requisition of their food stocks. When the army emerged from the Masovian forests in mid-January it left a wasteland of destroyed villages

A halt east of Posen until late October allowed new recruits to swell the size of the Swedish army to 44,000 men. Menshikov used this time to entrench behind the River Vistula around Warsaw. Once frost had improved the roads, Charles moved his army to the Vistula north of Menshikov, and behind it. A Swedish colonel said of the march, 'much of the populace were massacred, and everything standing burnt and laid waste, so I believe those who survived will not quickly forget the Swedes.' (Swedish Colonel Gyllenstierna, quoted in Englund, 1992).

Tsar Peter met Menshikov at Grodno and, finding the Russian forces insufficient to block the Swedish advance, gave orders to continue the retreat, the army screened by Menshikov's dragoons and Cossacks. On 28 January 1708, Charles entered Grodno, where his escort beat off a cavalry raid. The main Russian army meanwhile fell back towards the Lithuanian/Russian border, devastating the countryside as it went.

The Swedish advance continued until early February, when the army encamped around the Lithuanian town of Smorgoni. During this halt, the king held a meeting with General Lewenhaupt, the commander of the Swedish army in Livonia, ordering him to join him on the Russian border with 12,000 men and a full supply train by mid-summer. This requirement was forced on Charles by the Russian scorched-earth policy and the inhospitable terrain. By mid-March, food shortages forced the Swedes to move to Radovskoviche, near Minsk, where supplies were less scarce. The army

▼*Military flintlock pistols, early eighteenth century. The two top weapons were produced in Holland and the lower in France, all three being typical of those imported into Russia for the use of officers during Tsar Peter's reign. Highly decorated pieces such as these were seldom produced by Russian gunsmiths, whose brief was to mass-produce munition quality weapons. (State Museums of the Moscow Kremlin)*

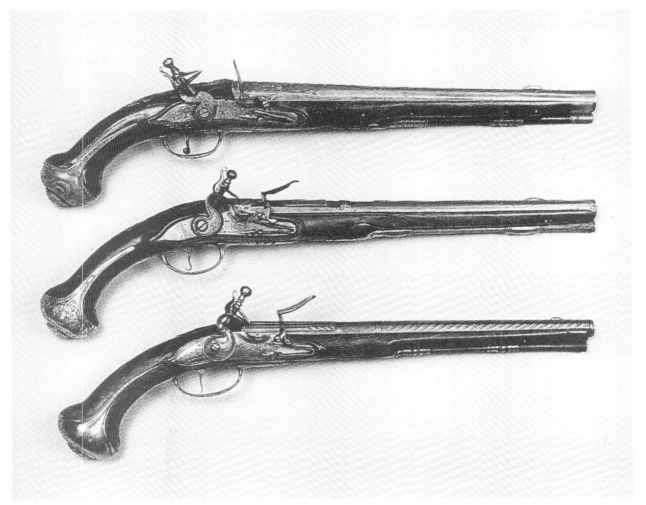

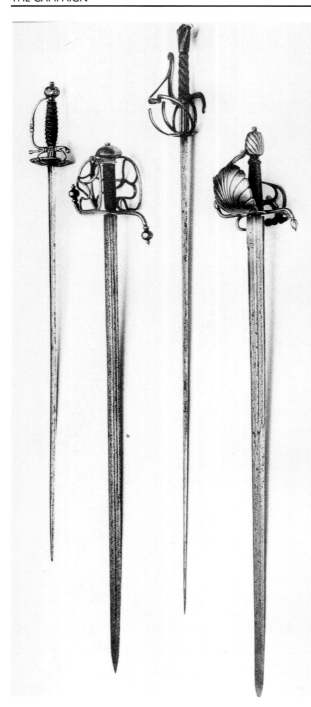

◀ *Four Swedish military swords, c.1709. The example on the left is a small-sword of the type carried by both officers and soldiers in the Swedish army, those of the former being more embellished. The second is a cavalry broad-sword, similar to the English or Scottish pattern; the third is again a late seventeenth century officer's sword of German origin; while the right-hand weapon is perhaps more representative of the type of weapon carried by a Swedish trooper. All of these examples were captured at Poltava. (State Museums of the Moscow Kremlin)*

The 'River Gate'

During the first weeks of June 1708, the two armies faced each other in cantonments awaiting Charles XII's order to restart the campaign. The Swedish army was strung out between Grodno and Radoskoviche, while the Russians held the line from Polotsk on the Dvina to Mogilev on the Dniepr, with the bulk of the army standing behind the Berezina – 35,000 Swedes facing 50,000 Russians. Although the Swedish army could be concentrated at a decisive point as the Russian command had to guard against possible threats to both Moscow and St. Petersburg, their army was far more dispersed, and the heavily forested terrain hindered any rapid redeployment. Peter was in the north organising the defence of the St. Petersburg approaches, while the direct road to Moscow was placed in the hands of Count Sheremetiev.

Count Piper, Charles XII's first minister, advocated a swing north towards Novgorod and St. Petersburg, which would secure the Baltic provinces and reverse all of Tsar Peter's military achievements. The King decided instead to drive eastwards through the 'river gate' towards Moscow. Tentative peace offers from the Tsar were rejected; Charles replying, 'I will treat with the Tsar in Moscow.' Peter is said to have quipped, 'My brother Charles wishes always to play the part of Alexander, but I flatter myself that he will not find in me another Darius.' (Voltaire, 1731)

The geography of the new campaigning area has been succinctly described by Jackson: 'It had now become clear to Peter that Charles was making for Moscow via the "river gate" between the upper reaches of the Dvina and Dniepr, and not for the

remained there for three months, drilling, gathering information and supplies, and preparing for the campaign ahead.

One final preparation was to leave a garrison of 5,000 men in Poland to prop up the Polish government of King Stanislaus in Charles's absence. This reduced the army to 38,000 men.

From the 'River Gate' to Poltava, 1708–9

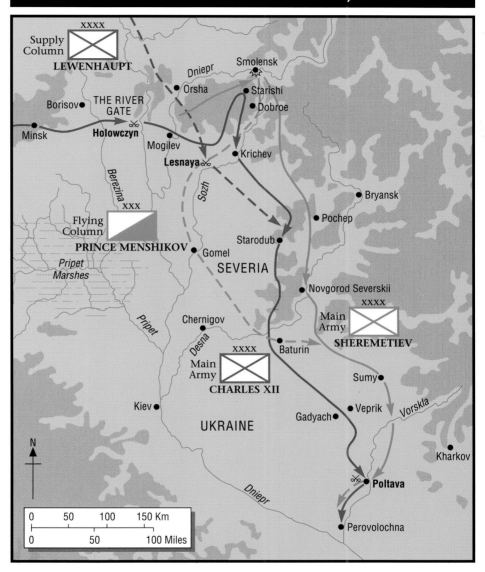

Baltic States. He, therefore, put in hand the defence of the numerous streams that cut across the path of the Swedish advance. A glance at the map will show that the great rivers Dvina and Dniepr provide an almost complete water barrier along the frontier of the older Russian lands from the Baltic to the Black Sea. Unfortunately the obstacle is incomplete in the centre. Both rivers as they approach each other turn eastwards towards Moscow leaving a narrow corridor undefended by either river. In this gateway lies the old frontier town of Smolensk, and through this gap runs the main highway to Moscow. Although

neither the Dvina nor Dniepr close this gate, several of their tributaries run north and south across it, and can be used as defensive positions to check an advance through the gap. The largest of these streams is the Berezina, of evil memory for Frenchmen in 1812, which together with the Ulla forms the best obstacle across the River Gate.' (W. G. F. Jackson, 1957)

On 6 June 1708, Charles marched from Radoskoviche towards the Berezina. A Russian advance guard of 8,000 cavalrymen waited behind the river at Borisov, where the Moscow road crossed

◀ *Count Axel Sparre (1652–1728) was a Major General of infantry in the Swedish army since being promoted from the rank of regimental colonel in 1705. Attached to the main Royal army throughout Charles XII's Polish and Russian campaigns, he led one of the four infantry columns at Poltava. After the surrender of the army he escaped with Charles XII to Bender in Turkey (Royal Armouries)*

the Berezina, these troopers forming the division of General Goltz. Passing through Minsk, Charles sent a detachment under Major General Axel Sparre towards Borisov to pin Goltz, while Charles swung his main army south along tracks through the heavy rain-sodden forests, reaching the river on 15 June. A screen of Russian dragoons and Cossacks were forced back, pontoon bridges were placed over the river, and the army crossed with little hindrance.

An attempt to outflank Goltz was hampered by incessant rain and muddy roads, allowing the Russians to withdraw behind the next river line, the Drut. This time Charles pinned Goltz with his main force while he led Sparre's advance guard to the north, crossed the river unopposed and so outflanked Goltz again. Once more appalling rain and mud held up the advance on Goltz's flank, allowing the Russians to disengage.

By 30 June, Charles had reached the Vabitch, a rain-swollen tributary of the Drut. Opposite his position near the village of Holowczyn, Charles could see extensive defensive works – clearly the main line of defence of the Russian army. This time no clear means of outflanking the position presented itself, and as more of the army arrived, Charles planned his forthcoming battle.

Holowczyn

The Russian positions behind the north–south axis of the Vabitch were commanded by Count Sheremetiev and consisted of three ad-hoc infantry divisions: that commanded directly by Sheremetiev in the centre (18 battalions), with those of General Hallart on his right (16 battalions) and Prince Repnin on his left (24 battalions). To the left of Repnin's position stood Goltz's cavalry division of about 6,500 men in three brigades, plus some 1,500 Cossacks. Each division, including the cavalry, was accompanied by a small train of artillery.

Once the screen of Russian dragoons was cleared from Holowczyn village, Charles spent the time waiting for the main body of his army by reconnoitring the Russian positions, accompanied by his aide, Gylenkrok, and his artillery commander, Bunow. He discovered that between Sheremetiev's and Repnin's divisions was a marsh, which the Russians clearly regarded as impassable since the sector remained undefended. This point Charles regarded as the key to the defence, and he drew up plans to exploit the gap. By making a surprise crossing of the Vabitch opposite the marsh he planned to struggle through it and, on reaching the firm ground beyond, turn to his right and roll up Repnin's right flank. This would be an infantry attack, supported by Bunow's artillery from the friendly bank. The Swedish cavalry could then cross to protect the infantry from Goltz's cavalry. During the evening of 3 July, Bunow brought his guns up, siting them on a low rise facing Repnin's entrenchments and to the south of the chosen crossing point.

The Swedish encampment was ordered to stand to at midnight, and the troops marched the two and a half miles to the river in darkness and torrential rain. A short Lutheran service was held en route while the artillery pieces were being dragged into position. Both the guns and two pontoon bridges carried by guardsmen proved difficult to move through the mud, and the pontoons were eventually abandoned. The troops arrived at the crossing points by dawn, only to be met by Russian sentries who fired warning shots to alert their compatriots. The time was now 2 a.m. Bunow's artillery opened up immediately, concentrating its fire on the right of Repnin's line. Any delay would now imperil the

▲ *Prince Nikita Repnin (1688–1726) was a Russian divisional commander from 1700 onwards. His poor performance at the Battle of Holowczyn led to his court martial.*

Despite this, he was given command of a division of infantry at Poltava, which he handled with a greater degree of competence. (Lenin Library, Moscow)

attack. The Lifeguard and Dalcarian Regiments formed the vanguard of the Swedish column, so Charles immediately led them through the chest-deep water. After forming with difficulty on the boggy far bank, the Swedes began to advance through the marsh. Meanwhile, fascines were laid on the river banks to assist the cavalry's crossing. Both the engineers and the Swedish vanguard began to be targeted by Repnin's artillery.

Prince Repnin sent appeals for assistance to both Sheremetiev and Goltz when the alarm was first raised, and he moved a number of battalions and guns to his right flank to contain the Swedes. Fearing that the Swedish move might be a diversion, he ordered the rump of his division to remain facing their unengaged front. After firing several volleys,

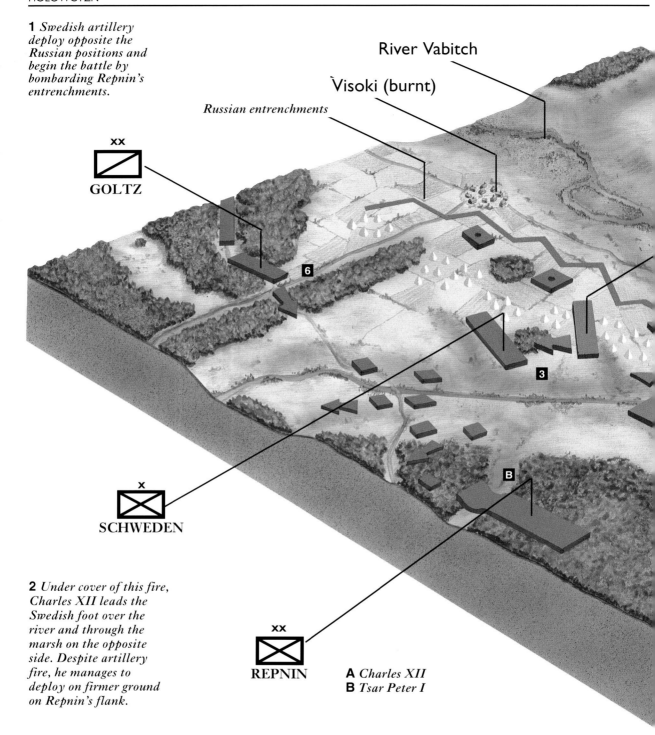

1 *Swedish artillery deploy opposite the Russian positions and begin the battle by bombarding Repnin's entrenchments.*

River Vabitch

Visoki (burnt)

Russian entrenchments

xx
GOLTZ

6

3

x
SCHWEDEN

B

2 *Under cover of this fire, Charles XII leads the Swedish foot over the river and through the marsh on the opposite side. Despite artillery fire, he manages to deploy on firmer ground on Repnin's flank.*

xx
REPNIN

A *Charles XII*
B *Tsar Peter I*

THE BATTLE OF HOLOWCZYN

The Swedes turn Repnin's line. Situation about dawn, as the Russians start to withdraw, 3 July 1708, as seen from the north-east

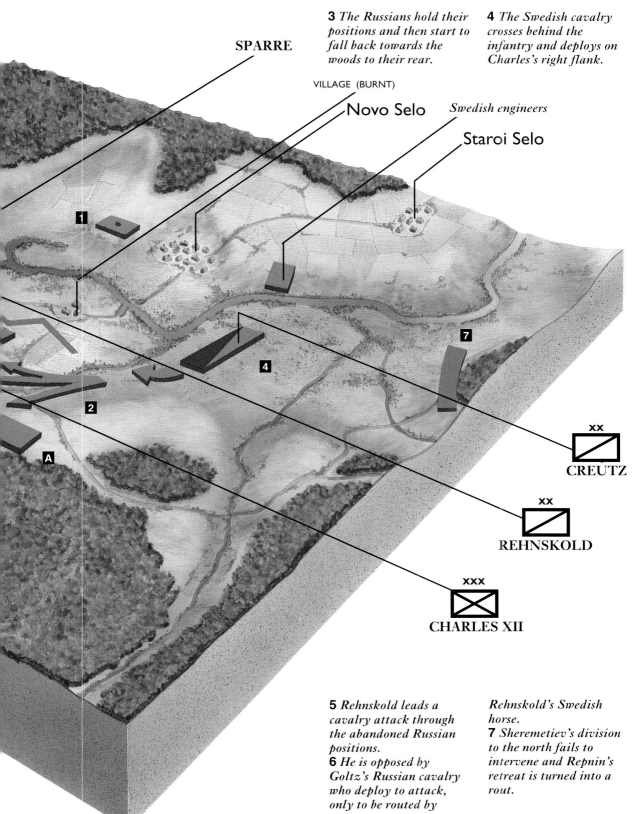

3 *The Russians hold their positions and then start to fall back towards the woods to their rear.*

4 *The Swedish cavalry crosses behind the infantry and deploys on Charles's right flank.*

SPARRE

VILLAGE (BURNT)

Novo Selo

Swedish engineers

Staroi Selo

CREUTZ

REHNSKOLD

CHARLES XII

5 *Rehnskold leads a cavalry attack through the abandoned Russian positions.*
6 *He is opposed by Goltz's Russian cavalry who deploy to attack, only to be routed by*

Rehnskold's Swedish horse.
7 *Sheremetiev's division to the north fails to intervene and Repnin's retreat is turned into a rout.*

the Russian right retired ahead of the Swedish van-guard. The Russian line was now disorganised and in danger of being rolled up from the flank, so Rep-nin ordered a withdrawal into the woods behind his position. Jefferyes wrote, 'The battle grew hott, so that in whole hours time nothing was heard but a continuall firing from the musquetry on both sides... the ennemy discharged commonly their guns at 30 or 40 paces distance, then runn, rallied and so discharg'd, which running fight lasted till 7

▲ Cavalry skirmish between Russians and Swedes. This is perhaps a fair indication of the state of an engagement after both sides made con-tact, where both swords and pistols would be employed. Normally, it was expected that a Swedish chevron forma-tion would either break a defending unit or smash it through sheer momentum and cohesion. (Engraving by Larmessain after the painting by Martin the Younger, early eighteenth century; State Historical Museum, Moscow)

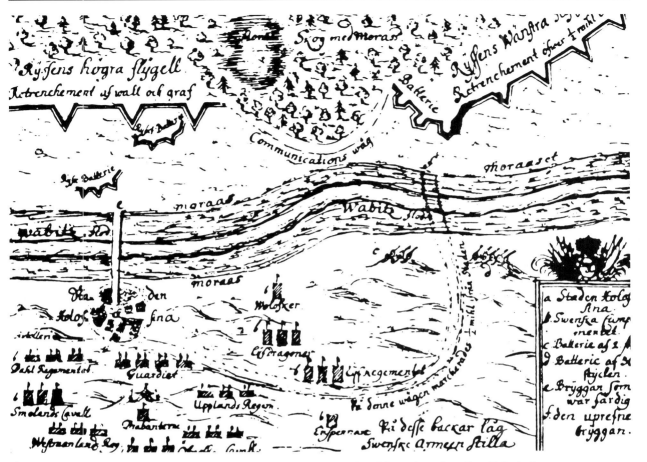

▲ *Plan of the battlefield of Holowczyn, 1708. This rather inaccurate Swedish engraving lists the Swedish regiments shown on their approach march, and the general dispositions of the Russian line,* *separated by a morass. It also depicts the Swedish artillery positions, sited on a small rise facing Repnin's entrenchments. (Swedish news pamphlet, 1708; author's collection)*

o'clock.' This confused fire-fight continued among the trees until pressure and lack of ammunition forced the Russians from the field.

Any chance of controlling Repnin's troops was lost as the defenders began to melt away into the forest. Six Swedish battalions led by Sparre swept through the line of entrenchments and fought off a Russian counter-attack led by General Schweden, who was mortally wounded in the engagement. A further Russian brigade of six battalions under General Renne from Sheremetiev's division arrived on the northern fringe of the marsh but could do no more than cover the retreat of Repnin's troops.

At this point the Swedish infantry were scattered amongst the woods and entrenchments, vulnerable to counter-attack. As the first Swedish cavalry forded the river, the leading brigade of Goltz's cavalry division (Ilfland's brigade) emerged from the woods on the southern edge of the battlefield. Ilfland's two regiments bore down on the Swedish infantry around the entrenchments to be met by two squadrons of the Swedish Household dragoon regiment. In the ensuing mêlée the Swedes were heavily outnumbered and in danger of being overwhelmed, when the Drabants arrived, followed by the Household cavalry regiment and elements of the Småland cavalry regiment. The outclassed Russian dragoons broke and ran south, pursued by the Swedish cavalry led by Rehnskold. The second Russian dragoon brigade (Heinske's) was disordered by the fugitives before being routed in their turn by the Swedes. Rehnskold swept on with his cavalry, falling upon the final Russian dragoon brigade commanded by the Prince of Hesse-Darm-

stadt as it emerged from the forest. This was cut to pieces before it had time to deploy from column of march.

The defeat of Goltz's cavalry was complete, but pursuit was hampered by the trees, and survivors of the Russian horse managed to escape largely unscathed. An attempt by Sheremetiev to relieve the pressure on Repnin by advancing over the Vabitch came to naught when the brigade-sized force was stopped by the West Bothnian Regiment outside Holowczyn village.

Confusion in the Swedish ranks meant that Charles was unable to exploit his victory by moving on Sheremetiev's position. Finding his army exposed with a hostile force on his flank, Sheremetiev withdrew his divisions in good order. This effectively ended the battle, leaving the Swedes in undisputed possession of the battlefield. Russian casualties were reported to have been 977 killed and 675 wounded. Although the Swedes only lost 267 killed on the field, many of the 1,000 wounded were to die through lack of medical attention. The majority of Swedish losses were concentrated in the Guard formations – men Charles could ill afford to lose. Holowczyn proved to be a phyrric victory indeed. The battle had not proved decisive, but it had at least opened the 'river gate', and the road to Moscow seemingly lay open.

The Long Road South

On 7 July, Charles XII entered Mogilev, 'one of the Kings of Poland oeconomyes, pretty large and surrounded with an old wall...' Although bridges were laid over the Dniepr, Charles remained in the town for four weeks without crossing into Russia. His army rested and gathered food, while Charles awaited the arrival of General Lewenhaupt and his supply column. Farther down the Moscow road, the Russian army retrenched itself around Gorki, and the Tsar took over overall direction of the army.

Lewenhaupt had left Livonia in late June, but bad weather and roads had delayed his advance. Although Charles's supply situation was not yet critical, further operations were limited until this column caught up. Meanwhile, the departure of that column from Livonia allowed Tsar Peter to recall General Bauer's division, which had been screening

▲ *Russian line grenadier, c. 1708–9. By the start of the campaign, Russia had grouped the grenadiers from her infantry regiments into permanent two-battalion regiments. In addition to the grenadier's mitre worn by* the figure, the illustration shows examples of the mitre worn by guard grenadiers. (Drawing by S. Hart. First reproduced in *Eighteenth Century Notes and Queries*, published by Partisan Press, UK)

the route from Livonia to St. Petersburg. When the Swedes eventually broke camp and crossed the Dniepr during the first week of August, there was still no news of Lewenhaupt. Charles marched south-east to Stalka, in an attempt to turn the Gorki fortifications and at the same time to cover Lewenhaupt's approach route. The Russian 'scorched-earth' policy and avoidance of open battle continued.

By 21 August the Swedes had reached Chernikov on the River Sozh, where for a week they remained, facing sizeable Russian forces on the far bank. Following the Swedish march south, Peter had abandoned the Gorki position, so when Charles turned north again on 23 August the road to Smolensk lay open. Peter had to force-march his troops north again to block the Swedish advance, and by the time the Swedes reached Malatitze they found a sizeable Russian force sited behind a marsh astride the route to Smolensk. In Jefferyes's account, 'the ennemy had sett out severall posts on horseback by the side of a morass, and perciev'd soon after their whole army encamp'd by a wood, having the said morass before them, which covered their front and both wings'. The Swedes made camp facing them.

During the night of 31 August, a Russian force of 4,000 dragoons and 9,000 infantry crossed the marsh under cover of a thick mist and attacked two isolated Swedish regiments on the right of the Swedish encampment. The Russians withdrew when Charles brought up reinforcements, leaving around 700 dead on the battlefield; the Swedes lost nearly 300 men. Charles's hope that this would be the precursor to a larger engagement was unfulfilled, but this was less significant than another aspect of the engagement – the obvious improvement in the morale and training of the Russian soldiers. Jefferyes wrote, 'The Svedes must own the Muscovites have learnt their lesson much better than they had either at the battles of Narva and Fraustadt, and that they equall if not exceed the Saxons both in discipline and valour; 'tis true their cavalry is not able to cope with ours, but their infantry stand their ground obstinately, and 'tis a difficult matter to separate them or bring them into confusion if they be not attacked sword in hand.' Tsar Peter himself was pleased with the perfor-

▲ *Russian officer, c.1700–21. During the period of Peter the Great, considerable latitude was shown in the regulations for the uniform prescribed for officers. This figure is depicted wearing a coat resembling that of the infantrymen, with additional trimming. His sash would most likely have been in the national colours of white, blue and red. His status as an 'under-officer' is denoted by his partisan. (Drawing by S. Hart. First reproduced in* Eighteenth Century Notes and Queries, *published by Partisan Press, UK)*

▲*General Field Marshal Michail Golitsyn (1675–1730). As a divisional commander, he led the Russian attack at Malatitze (Dobroe) in August 1708, and he commanded the Guards at Poltava. (Portrait by an unknown artist, early eighteenth century; State Historical Museum, Moscow)*

▲*Josias Cederheilm (1673–1729); Secretary to Charles XII and Secretary (manager) of the Chancery in the Field during the campaign. He was captured at Poltava. (Painting by Lucas von Breda; Royal Armouries)*

mance of his troops: 'Since first I entered military service, I have never seen nor heard of our soldiers having kept up such a heavy fire, or maintained such order in their operations.'

Nevertheless, Peter continued his strategy of avoiding major battle, and his army melted into the woods again, protected by a screen of dragoons and Cossacks. On 4 September, Charles resumed his march, arriving in Tatarsk and Starishi on 4 September. En route, two major Russian division-sized cavalry raids caused further losses to the Swedish force. The second of these, at Rajovka on 10 September, resulted in the King and his escort being surrounded by seemingly overwhelming num-

bers of Russian dragoons for some time before they could be rescued.

On reaching Tartarsk, Charles was forced to consider the realities of his position. Food supplies were becoming critical, and scouts reported that ahead they 'found nothing but what was burnt and destroyed, and of large villages little left but the bare names, we had also news of the like destruction as far as Smolensko'. One witness reported that the smoke from burning villages hid the sun for days. Desertions from his army were mounting, and there was still no firm news of Lewenhaupt's supply column, which would be needed to cross the scorched landscape. Consequently, the King made the decision to head south, abandoning the advance along the Smolensk-Moscow axis. His main aim now would be to keep his army alive, by beating the Russians to the undamaged region of Severia. General Langercrona was sent with an advance guard of 3,000 men to secure the route, and the main army marched south on 15 September.

From the start, things went badly wrong for Charles. In order to secure Severia, the Swedes needed to capture three fortified towns: Mglin, Pochep and Starodub. Mglin was taken without a fight, but Langercrona missed the road to Pochep and, finding himself outside Starodub, retraced his steps rather than seizing the opportunity to capture it – claiming that such a move was not in his orders. Russian dragoons under Ilfland quickly occupied and garrisoned Starodub and Mglin, and the opportunity was lost.

The Swedish army encamped around Mglin to recover from its long march south while awaiting news of Lewenhaupt's force. Losses had been severe, the army now barely numbering 25,000 men. Jefferyes reported that, 'the late march His Majesty made... has been through vast woods and wildernesses, and must have cost His Majesty dear... 'tis thought we have lost more in this ramble than if we had given the enemy a battle.'

By 6 October, news of Lewenhaupt's force at last reached the King. It was not what he had hoped to hear.

Lesnaya

When Charles XII left Tatarsk on 15 September, Lewenhaupt was still 30 miles west of the Dniepr, 90 miles from the main Swedish army. Peter planned to exploit the gap between the two forces. General Sheremetiev was given command of the main Russian army and ordered to shadow Charles, keeping between him and Moscow. Peter took direct command of a *korvolan* (flying column) of ten battalions of his most experienced infantry, which were

▲ Russian infantry unit in line, c.1709. Although this engraving erroneously depicts the Russian battalion formed into five rather than four ranks and omits to represent the pikemen, it gives a fair representation of a contemporary battle formation. The unit is meant to represent a battalion, although it is portrayed as a strong company. Note the position of officers to the front and sergeants to the rear of the unit. (Detail from engraving by Nicolas de Larmessin; State Hermitage Museum, St. Petersburg)

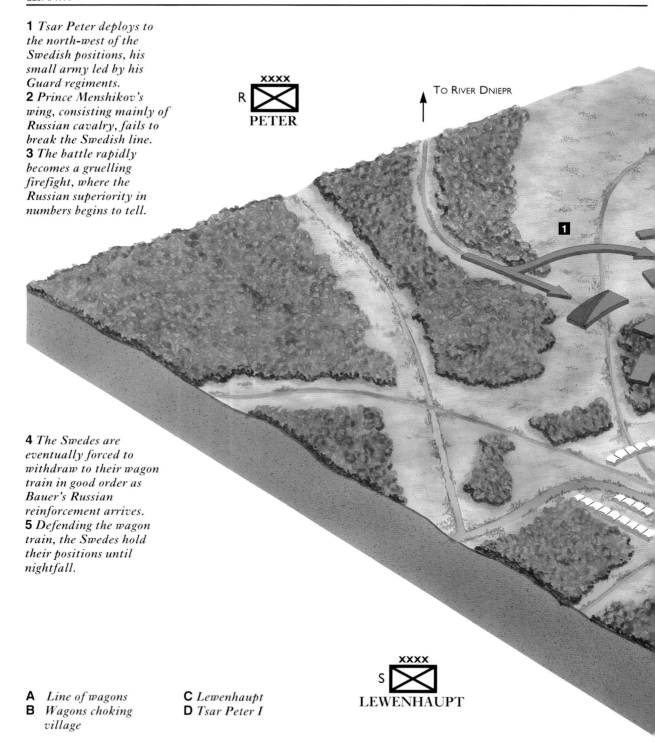

1 *Tsar Peter deploys to the north-west of the Swedish positions, his small army led by his Guard regiments.*
2 *Prince Menshikov's wing, consisting mainly of Russian cavalry, fails to break the Swedish line.*
3 *The battle rapidly becomes a gruelling firefight, where the Russian superiority in numbers begins to tell.*

R ⊠ xxxx
PETER

TO RIVER DNIEPR

1

4 *The Swedes are eventually forced to withdraw to their wagon train in good order as Bauer's Russian reinforcement arrives.*
5 *Defending the wagon train, the Swedes hold their positions until nightfall.*

S ⊠ xxxx
LEWENHAUPT

A Line of wagons
B Wagons choking village
C Lewenhaupt
D Tsar Peter I

THE BATTLE OF LESNAYA

The initial Russian attack on the Swedish positions, mid-afternoon, 29 September 1708, as seen from the south-east

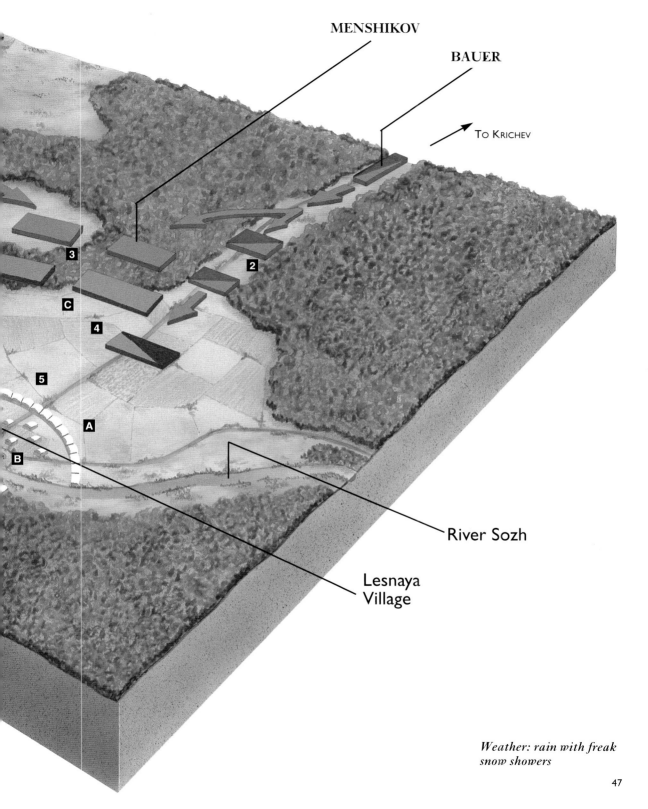

To MOGILEV

MENSHIKOV

BAUER

To KRICHEV

3

2

C

4

5

A

B

River Sozh

Lesnaya
Village

*Weather: rain with freak
snow showers*

▲ *Tsar Peter I on horse-back. Note the unadorned uniform of a Guard Colonel worn by the monarch. The engraving is set at the moment of victory: troopers in the foreground are shown 'mopping up' at the close* of *the battle, while a messenger brings confirmation that the Swedes are beaten. (Engraving by Martin the Younger, early eighteenth century; State Historical Museum, Moscow)*

▼ *Tsar Peter I at the Battle of Lesnaya, 1708. The wooded nature of the battlefield is shown, although the village of Lesnaya seen in the background is sited at the end of an area of open fields. Several stages of the bat-* *tle are depicted here. (Painting by Martin the Younger, early eighteenth century; The State Artillery Museum, St. Petersburg)*

▶ *Full-dress uniform of a Colonel of the Preobrazhenski Guard Regiment, c. 1720–25. This example belonged to* *Tsar Peter I. The sash colours are white, blue and red (State Historic Museum, Moscow)*

mounted on horses, ten regiments of dragoons and four batteries of horse artillery (a uniquely Russian formation at that time). The force totalled 11,625 men. An additional 3,000 dragoons under General Bauer were ordered to join the *korvolan* as soon as possible.

Lewenhaupt's column comprised 7,500 infantry and 5,000 cavalry and dragoons. These provided the escort for a supply column off almost 1,000 wagons. Lewenhaupt reached the Dniepr on 18 September, where he received news of the King's march south, together with orders to join him. His column took a week to cross, when, sensing the presence of the Tsar's force, he ordered a forced march to the River Sozh and the relative safety of the Severia. When the Russian dragoons caught up on 27 September he sent the wagons on ahead and despatched 3,000 cavalry to secure the Sozh crossing at Propoitsk. Following a running skirmish, dawn found his army outside the village of Lesnaya, with the Russians deploying in the woods to the north and east.

Lewanhaupt deployed his main line to the north of the village at the edge of the woods. Behind them and to their right, the Swedish cavalry waited to exploit any weakness in the Russian dispositions and to protect the right flank from envelopment. Prince Menshikov, with 7 dragoon regiments and 3 battalions of infantry, deployed on the Russian left flank, while the Tsar, commanding the main line of the 2 Guard regiments and 1 battalion of infantry, took the right flank. The reserve of 3 dragoon regiments was also commanded by the Tsar. The main battle lines clashed around 1 p.m., and a fierce fire-fight raged in the woods to the north of Lesnaya. In mid-afternoon Menshikov attempted to exploit a gap between the Swedish lines created by the wooded terrain, but he was stopped by the Swedish cavalry. Russian infantrymen sought cover in the woods, and a spirited Swedish infantry attack almost broke Menshikov's troops. Seeing the developing crisis, Peter sent the Semenovsky Guard Regiment into a counter-attack, which propped up the Russian line. The Tsar in his journal records that 'all day it was

impossible to see where victory would lie'. Just after 4 p.m., General Bauer's dragoons arrived, and these were launched upon the Swedish right flank. This fresh development forced the Swedes to withdraw in good order to the protection of earthworks thrown up around the village. The return of the 3,000 Swedish horse recalled from Propoitsk stabilised the Swedish line and relieved pressure on the main Swedish infantry line, which was struggling to hold the area around the village. The battle was still

Battle of Lesnaya, 1708 (Phase 1)

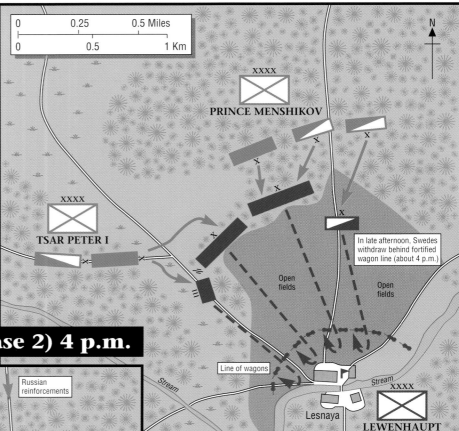

0   0.25   0.5 Miles

0   0.5   1 Km

N

XXXX
PRINCE MENSHIKOV

XXXX
TSAR PETER I

In late afternoon, Swedes withdraw behind fortified wagon line (about 4 p.m.)

Open fields

Open fields

Line of wagons

Stream

Stream

Lesnaya

XXXX
LEWENHAUPT

Lesnaya (Phase 2) 4 p.m.

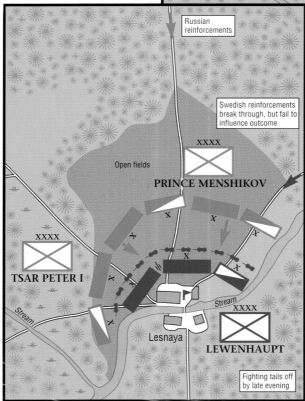

Russian reinforcements

Swedish reinforcements break through, but fail to influence outcome

Open fields

XXXX
PRINCE MENSHIKOV

XXXX
TSAR PETER I

Stream

Stream

Lesnaya

XXXX
LEWENHAUPT

Fighting tails off by late evening

continuing at 8 p.m. when dusk and an unseasonable snow shower brought the battle to a close.

Both forces were in little position to continue the battle the next day, but Lewenhaupt considered that his position was untenable. He ordered that the supply column be burnt and the artillery pieces buried in the banks of the stream behind the village. At this point Swedish morale broke. As the wagons burned through the night and troops plundered the stores they had escorted from Livonia, the remains of Lewenhaupt's force began a ragged retreat towards the river. Order was soon lost during the night march through the trees, and by the time the Swedish army reached the river bank it was little more than a disorganised mass. Finding the bridges burnt at Propoitsk, the troops milled aimlessly

▲ *Detail of fighting during the Battle of Lesnaya (1708). A battle line of Russian infantry and dismounted dragoons in the foreground are attempting to repel a Swedish counter-attack. Russian dragoon reinforcements are moving up in the foreground. The units in the background represent positions during a later stage of the battle. (Detail of the painting by Martin the Younger, early eighteenth century; State Artillery Museum, St. Petersburg)*

▶ *Another detail of the same painting; the scene now represents the later stages of the battle, when the Swedish line shown in the background has been pushed back to the baggage train surrounding the* village of Lesnaya, while by now superior numbers of Russian troops have moved up and are engaging them. (Detail of the painting by Martin the Younger, early eighteenth century; State Artillery Museum, St. Petersburg)

▲ *Silver medal awarded to participants after the Battle of Lesnaya, 1708. The obverse portrays Tsar Peter I riding in triumph over a trophy of captured Swedish arms; the reverse displays a map of the battlefield over the title 'Glorious Victory at Lesnaya'. (State Historical Museum, Moscow)*

around the river, and as dawn arrived, so did the Cossacks. Some 500 Swedes were cut down in the ensuing fight, the remainder either fleeing into the woods or surrendering.

Morning revealed the full scale of the disaster. When Lewenhaupt rallied his shattered troops a few miles farther down the Sozh, his force had been reduced by half; the Swedes had lost 607 cavalry, 751 dragoons, 4,449 infantry – of these, nearly 3,000 had been captured by the Russians – all their artillery and the whole 1,000-wagon supply train.

Lewenhaupt led the stragglers in the footsteps of the King, and ten days later the two Swedish forces at last combined when Lewenhaupt found the King's encampment. Charles had only heard of the defeat two days earlier, when his scouts contacted the lost column. On the same day, the sounds of celebration were heard in nearby Russian outposts. Tsar Peter was overjoyed: 'This victory may be called our first, for we have never had one like it over regular troops, and then with numbers inferior to those of the enemy. Truly it was the cause of all

the subsequent good fortune of Russia and it put heart into our men, and was the mother of the Battle of Poltava.' Massie summed up the summer campaign when he said of Charles, 'Having waited too long for Lewenhaupt, in the end he had not waited long enough.' (Massie, 1981)

Race for the Ukraine

It has been suggested that Charles XII's aim once the army had recovered from its summer campaign was to march from Severia towards Moscow along the Kaluga road, the second main artery leading to the Russian capital. Lesnaya now made such a move impractical. One other strategy lay open. The *hetman* (leader) of the Ukrainian Cossacks, Mazeppa, had just declared himself for Charles, leading his people in open revolt against the Tsar. Although many of his countrymen retained their allegiance to the Tsar, he had enough support to open another window of opportunity for Charles. Jefferyes reports that on the day following the news of Lesnaya the King wrote to Mazeppa promising his support and requesting the provision of winter quarters in the Ukraine. With a friendly populace and plentiful supplies, the Ukraine was seen as 'a country flowing with milk and honey'. The plan was now to winter the army in the Ukraine and to attack Moscow from the south in the spring. Charles was also hoping to gain Ukrainian recruits and receive reinforcements from Poland; and Turkey might enter the war against Russia. In order to succeed, speed was vital. The race for the Ukraine was on.

By 11 October the Swedish army was moving south towards Mazeppa's capital, Baturin. Ilfland, commanding the Russian advance guard, fought a number of skirmishes en route, at Novgorod Severskii and during the Swedish crossing of the River Desna. The latter, undertaken on 2 November, was carried out in the face of a division-sized Russian blocking force.

With the Swedes only four miles away, Prince Menshikov arrived at Baturin with a *korvolan*, and captured the fortress town by storm. The town was burnt and its large magazine of food, fodder and ammunition destroyed before Menshikov retired. Charles's Ukrainian ally now had nothing to offer Charles but his fealty and the reinforcements of his dwindling number of followers. Any prospect Mazeppa had of an independent Ukrainian state was now reliant on the success and benevolence of the Swedish king.

By mid-November the Swedish army was encamped around the charred ruins of Baturin gathering in supplies before the onset of winter. With local help the Swedes beat the Russians to the fortified towns of Romny, Gadyach and Lokhvitsa to the south of Baturin, and by the end of the month Charles's army had settled into winter quarters in and around the towns. Regiments were dispersed throughout the area. The Russians themselves went into winter quarters to the east, blocking the road to Moscow via Kursk and Orel. Russian patrols started to harry the Swedish camps as the war settled down into a pattern of raids and skirmishes fought with bitter ferocity in freezing conditions.

▼ *Russian cavalry longarms: a shortened musket and a carbine. Both use the 'french-lock' flintlock mechanism. In general, Russian dragoons made extensive use of the shortened musket, whose clumsiness when used* *mounted was compensated for by the increased range and accuracy it offered. (Drawings by the author; originals in the collection of the State Historical Museum, Moscow)*

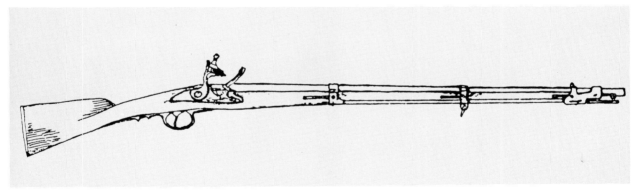

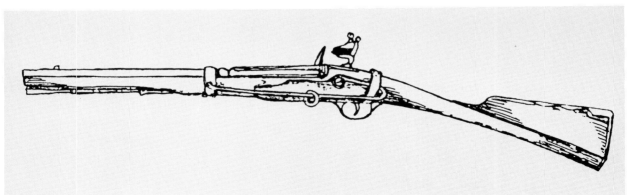

*Russians at Lesnaya. Kneeling front and standing
centre, Troopers of the Vladimirski Dragoon Regiment; left, firing, and background, Troopers of the
Moskoviski Dragoon Regiment; right, Captain,
Moskoviski Regiment. (Painting by David Rickman)*

Ukrainian Winter

The winter of 1708/9 came early. It was to be the worst in living memory. Birds froze in the trees, and riders and horses died as one frozen mass. The only protection from the icy wind in the empty Ukrainian landscape were the few towns and villages, which became fought over with a ruthlessness brought on by the need to survive. Despite the conditions, both monarchs saw advantages in continuing the fighting.

Charles's main aim was to ensure the safety of his winter quarters by ejecting the Russians from the settlements west of the River Vorskla, which would give him a secure territorial boundary. Peter wanted to contain the Swedes and to pre-empt any drive on Kharkov and Kursk, the road to Moscow. To this end he established garrisons in a number of towns bordering the Swedish area, including Veprik and Poltava. Not content with a passive containment, he also launched a number of raids on

▲ *Detail of the entry of Russian troops into Moscow after Poltava. Note the display of all the established trophies of war of the time – artillery pieces, drums, standards, wounded senior enemy officers and regimental pay wagons. (Engraving by A. Zubov, 1711; State Historical Museum, Moscow)*

Swedish-held settlements. On 19 December the Russians launched an attack on Gadyach, forcing Charles to gather his army and march to relieve the town. The approach was made through deep snow in atrocious conditions, with men freezing to death by the roadside. When they arrived three days later they found the Russians had withdrawn, leaving the Swedes to seek what shelter they could in the now overcrowded town.

To prevent further incursions, Charles decided to attack Veprik, the Russian-held Cossack fort a few miles to the east of Gadyach. The fort was sited on a hill outside the village of the same name. The garrison was commanded by Ferber (a mis-spelling

◀ *Baron Carl Gustav Roos (1655–1722), Major General of Infantry in the Swedish army. He commanded one of the four attacking infantry columns at Poltava, and his obsession to capture the third redoubt led to his force being cut off from the main army and destroyed. His actions reduced the Swedish infantry force by a third prior to their main attack. He was captured with the remains of his command and died on his return from captivity. (Royal Armouries)*

of Fairbairn, a Scottish officer listed in the rolls of 1706), who had two foot battalions, 400 Cossacks and a couple of artillery pieces at his disposal. The defences had been strengthened by pouring water over the earthen ramparts, and this rapidly turned into ice. On 7 January after a surrender demand was rejected, the Swedes attacked, the operation commanded by Rehnskold. Six infantry and two dismounted dragoon regiments, 3,000 men in all, attacked in three columns, supported by artillery fire. This and a subsequent attack were driven off, accurate fire from Cossack hunting rifles picking off officers and ladder-carriers as they tried to scale the ice rampart. In the two hours before nightfall stopped the action, the Swedes lost 400 men killed and 600 wounded, including Rehnskold. The garri-

son itself was now out of ammunition, and surrendered with honour the following day. But the small action had cost the Swedish army dear. Charles was beginning to realise that the chance of receiving reinforcements from Poland was slim. Manpower was now becoming a problem.

The 1709 Campaign

In mid-January, Charles launched a further attack by raiding the towns of Krasnokutsk and Gorodno, driving out General Ronne's Russian dragoons after protracted skirmishing. A similar raid in late February saw the Swedes themselves adopting a 'scorched-earth' policy, burning Oposhnya on the River Vorskla, after Charles at the head of five cav-

▶*Count Arvid Bernard Horn (1675–1756), Swedish officer and King's councillor he commanded the Swedish Drabanten corps, the crack squadron of Swedish cavalry lifeguards, and carried the rank of Major General during the campaign. He fought at both Holowczyn and Poltava, and escaped to Turkey with Charles XII after the surrender of the army. (Royal Armouries)*

alry regiments had defeated Prince Menshikov with seven dragoon regiments in a running battle.

By March the Swedes had shifted their area of cantonment to the land between the Vorskla and the Psiol rivers, sitting astride the Kiev–Kharkov road; it was an ideal base for further operations. Settlements in their old area of operations were burnt to deny their use to the Russians. The main Russian army remained around Kharkov, with further forces to the east of the Vorskla.

During winter, Charles had been negotiating with both the Turks and the Zaporozhnian Cossacks in the search for new allies. Tsar Peter had managed to counter both moves, Tolstoy, the Russian ambassador, securing an armistice with the Turks, which tightened Charles's isolated position. Then, in April

and May, lightning Russian raids destroyed the river fleet and base of the Zaporozhnians on the lower Dniepr.

The coming of spring found the Swedes strung out along the Vorskla from Oposhnya to Poltava. While awaiting the reinforcements from Poland which he still expected, Charles decided to concentrate his army around Poltava, and, to secure his position prior to a drive north towards Kursk, he prepared to besiege the Russian garrison there. By this stage Prince Menshikov, commanding the Russian army in the Tsar's absence, had concentrated his forces on the eastern bank of the Vorskla opposite Poltava. It was now becoming clear that no Swedish reinforcements would be arriving that summer.

The siege trenches were begun by the Swedes on the night of 1 May, but the siege was conducted with considerable lethargy, so that by late June the small walled town had still not fallen. Skirmishes continued with Russian raiding units, and twice isolated Swedish units were badly cut up. During a visit to his outposts on the banks of the Vorskla on 17 June, Charles was hit in the foot by a musket ball. This demonstration of the King's vulnerability came as an unwelcome shock to his soldiers. He survived a fever following the subsequent operation, but for the next few weeks he would be unable to do more than dictate orders. The army would be deprived of his charismatic leadership at the time when they most needed it.

On 27 June, Jefferyes wrote, 'The beginning of the year has not been so successful for us as we

▲ Detail from the 'Battle of Poltava' mosaic by Mikhail Lomonsov, 1756. The Russian soldier dispatching the Swede is incorrectly dressed in the post-1720 pattern uniform of the Preobrazhenski Guards. (Academy of Sciences, St. Petersburg)

thought it would, the losses we have had at severall times, though not very considerable, yet are greater than we well can beare in the circumstances we now are.'

Tsar Peter had been attending to state business in Moscow, and when he arrived in the Russian camp in early June he decided to move the army to the western bank of the river. Following a failed attempt opposite Poltava during the night of 14 June, Peter looked for a crossing farther north. On the night of the 16th, following diversionary attacks lower down the river, a crossing was made at Petrovka, seven miles north of Poltava. The rapid con-

► *Artillery and mortars participating in the exercises of Tsar Peter's poteshne (play) regiments. All carriages are shown painted in an orange-red colour. The stylised fortification is typical of a redoubt of the period, such as those at Veprik and Poltava. (Watercolour from Krekshnin's History of Tsar Peter I; Lenin Library, Moscow)*

struction of a fortified camp and the incapacity of Charles meant that no attempt was made to throw the Russians back over the river, and during the next few days the whole Russian army was transferred to the west bank. The army then moved south, establishing itself in a new fortified camp with its rear resting on the bluffs above the Vorskla, only four miles from Poltava.

Because of the proximity of the two armies, a major engagement was now almost inevitable, and both sides prepared for the coming engagement. The scene was set for the decisive battle of the war.

◀ *Russian bombardier, c.1727–30. His cartridge box bears the monogram of Tsar Peter II (Peter the Great's grandson), but the uniform is similar to that worn by bombardiers at Poltava. He demonstrates the approved method of firing by resting the hand mortar on a specially issued halberd. (Hermitage Museum, St. Petersburg)*

▶ *A senior Russian officer during the Battle of Poltava, 1709. He probably represents Count Sheremetiev, accompanied by troopers of his personal escort, the 'General's Dragoon Company'. (Detail from Lomonsov's Poltava mosaic, 1756; Academy of Sciences, St. Petersburg)*

▶ *A further detail of the mosaic: a Russian dragoon and guard grenadier struggle with Swedish horsemen for control of a company standard. The artist has placed Charles XII and his litter beside the infantry fight raging in the background. In reality, the Swedish king took no direct control of the battle at Poltava. (Detail from Lomonsov's Poltava mosaic, 1756; Academy of Sciences, St. Petersburg)*

THE BATTLE

The Battlefield

The Russian fortified encampment backing on to the bluffs above the western bank of the River Vorskla was roughly rectangular in shape, but open at the rear, overlooking the river. An attacker had to cross a ditch protected by *chevaux de frise*, then mount a rampart (courtin), behind which was a firing step capable of housing artillery pieces. The earthen fortifications were built in the Vauban style, the courtin interspersed with triangular bastions and three entrances. The fort took up an area of approximately 1½ square kilometres. In front of the camp was a large steppe-like field of dry, sandy soil, stretching westwards for 1 kilometre. This merged into a wide strip of low-lying ground, running north–south; this could shield any troops occupying it from artillery fire from the camp. Behind this was Budyschenski wood, which curved away to the north-west, along the Ivanchintsi stream.

1½ kilometres north-west of the camp the plain ended in a marshy gully and stream known as the Great Ouvrage. A smaller patch of marsh lay in front of it, marking the end of the low-lying depression. The gully marked the northern boundary of the battle arena. Small groups of ruined cottages were located on the banks of both streams.

A hundred metres south of the fortified camp lay the Yakovetski Wood, an area of woodland, streams and gullies that bordered the Vorskla on its eastern side and extended west for up to 2 kilometres at its southern end. The woodland continued to the south for just over 4 kilometres, ending in a ridge overlooking the walls of Poltava, a kilometre farther south. A cloister sat on the end of the ridge, and this was used as Charles XII's headquarters before the battle. The northern end of the wood ended just past the camp, leaving an open area between Budyschenski and Yakovetski woods just over a kilometre wide. Both woods were largely impassable for ordered formations of troops, and the Russians had chopped down trees to enhance the natural barrier of the undergrowth.

The fortified town of Poltava itself was surrounded by Swedish siege works, the main approach trenches being on the north-western side of the town. Between the town and the river a kilo-

▼*A hand mortar as used by a Russian bombardier during the reign of Tsar Peter I. This seemingly impractical weapon had a bore of 49mm, and fired a small grenade. They were used for the close-range defence of artillery positions and continued to be used after the death of Tsar Peter (State Museums of the Moscow Kremlin)*

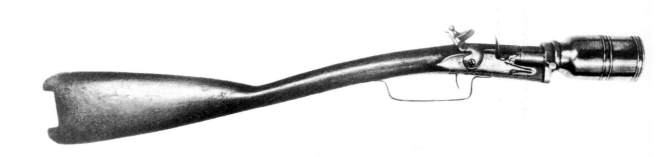

The Battle of Poltava: Initial Dispositions

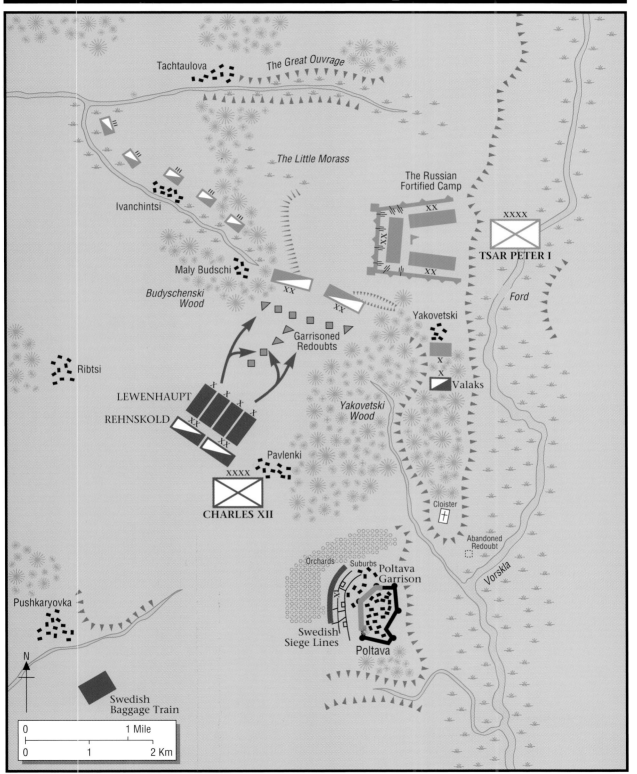

Tachtaulova

The Great Ouvrage

The Little Morass

Ivanchintsi

The Russian
Fortified Camp

XX

XXXX

TSAR PETER I

Maly Budschi

XX

XX

Ford

Budyschenski
Wood

Garrisoned
Redoubts

Yakovetski

Ribtsi

X

X

Valaks

LEWENHAUPT

x

x
x
x

x

x

Yakovetski
Wood

REHNSKOLD

XX

XX

Pavlenki

XXXX

Cloister

Abandoned
Redoubt

CHARLES XII

Vorskla

Orchards
Suburbs
Poltava
Garrison

Pushkaryovka

Swedish
Siege Lines
Poltava

N

Swedish
Baggage Train

0		1 Mile
0	1	2 Km

▲ *European troops constructing gabions as part of a defensive position, early eighteenth century. The technique of interleaving soaked small branches between a ring of upright stakes was a skilled process. The earth-filled result was impervious to all but the largest of artillery rounds. These would have been used by the Swedes to form their siege lines around Poltava. (French watercolour by an unknown artist; Royal Armouries).*

metre away to the east lay an area of marshy ground. A number of abandoned earthwork forts lined the marsh, remnants of Swedish positions when the Russians were considering a direct river crossing in that sector a week before. To the north-west of the outlying suburbs of the town lay an area of orchards, which led into a large open steppe, which extended for 4 kilometres as far as the hamlets of Ribtsi and Pushkaryovka, north-west and west of Poltava respectively.

During the evening of 27 June, the dispositions of the opposing sides were as follows.

The Russians deployed 25,500 infantry and 73 guns in their fortified camp. A small detachment of 1,000 foot and 1,000 Cossacks was posted in Yakovetski Wood to guard the southern approaches to the camp. In the gap between the two woods the Russians had built a line of six square or rectangular redoubts spaced no more than 150 metres apart to cover the open approach to the plain in front of the camp. Each redoubt was about 50 metres on each side, and consisted of a high parapet with a ditch in front of it, the ditch being surrounded by chevaux de frise.

In the centre of this line Peter had just begun the construction of a second line of four redoubts, extending south-west at right angles to the first line. The two farthest redoubts had still not been completed by dawn on 28 June. The rationale behind this extra line was that a roundshot fired from the main line could roll through the four ranks of a unit in line. If the line of new redoubts were bypassed by an attacker, the enemy unit could be enfiladed, and the same shot was capable (in theory) of hitting more than a hundred men. This placed an attacker in an unenviable situation: he must either disrupt his army by attacking the forts or else subject his troops to murderous crossfire. The redoubts were garrisoned by 4,000 infantry (8 battalions) and 16 guns. A screen of Cossacks lined the edge of Budyschenski Wood to give early warning of a flanking attack to the north of the redoubts.

The Swedish infantry were encamped in the orchards surrounding the cloisters north of Poltava, 8,200 men in 18 battalions. The main cavalry force of 7,800 cavalry was encamped on the plain to the west, near Ribtsi. The artillery and baggage trains were at Pushkaryovka, guarded by 2,000 cavalry and a number of Cossacks. The siegeworks around Poltava were garrisoned by a token force of 1,100 infantry (2 battalions) and a handful of dragoons and Cossacks. A further force of 1,800 cavalry was strung out below Poltava, guarding the banks of the Vorskla. The regiment of 1,000 irregular Polish Vallacks was posted in Yakovetski Wood, facing the Russian outposts there.

Through the Redoubts

When Charles XII was wounded on the eve of the battle, the Swedes were deprived of their charismatic and able leader – more than that, their talisman of victory. Although the King retained his nominal command of the army, direct control now devolved to Field Marshal Rehnskold. Rehnskold was also overall cavalry commander, while General Lewenhaupt commanded the infantry. The King had some degree of mobility, being carried on a stretcher by 24 guardsmen, who also acted as a human shield around the monarch.

The Swedish plan was simple. The army would form up during the night south of the Russian redoubts. Before dawn on 28 June, Lewenhaupt's infantry would move forward through the redoubt line, followed by the cavalry. The foot would then launch an attack on the Russians crammed inside their fortified camp while Rehnskold led the cavalry round to the north to block the Russian retreat, and to slaughter the fleeing enemy. Success depended upon a number of factors: that the Russians would remain immobile during the Swedish attack; that the redoubt line could be passed without excessive difficulty; that the Russian dragoons could be driven from the field; and that the Russian entrenchments could be stormed as they had been at Narva. The whole plan was based on the superiority of the Swedish army, the momentum of the attack and, above all, on surprise. If all went to plan, the triumphant slaughter of the Russian army at Narva could be repeated.

The Swedish infantry moved into position soon after midnight. Their starting lines were about a kilometre south of the first Russian redoubt, from which the sound of sawing and hammering could be heard. The 18 battalions were divided into four columns, supported by a battery of four regimental guns. There they waited for more than two hours for the cavalry to come up, so that dawn was already breaking by the time the whole army was ready. It was now clear that the late start put the element of surprise at risk. After conferring with his two principal commanders, the King decided to continue with the attack anyway. Rehnskold gave the word:

▶ *James William Bruce (1670–1735), General of Ordnance in the Russian army. He introduced a number of revolutionary innovations to the Russian artillery arm, including the use of horse artillery. During Poltava he commanded the main Russian gun line, situated within the fortified encampment. (Engraving by an anonymous German artist, c.1710; State Historical Museum, Moscow).*

▲ *Model of an early to mid-eighteenth century artillery piece and limber, in this case a bronze 12-pounder. Contemporary field carriages were still relatively immobile; so much so that artillery* played *little part in the Carolean doctrine of aggressive warfare. (Royal Artillery Institute, Woolwich)*

▼ *The Russian fortified camp at Poltava, with* Russian infantry and dragoons drawn up in the foreground. Note the formal arrangement of tents within the encampment. The village of Yakovetski is depicted in the background. (Detail from an *engraving by Larmessain after the painting by Martin the Younger, early eighteenth century; State Hermitage Museum, St. Petersburg)*

Unlike other European armies of the period, the Swedes did not group their grenadiers together in separate battalions. They were usually deployed on the flanks of the musketeers. (Painting by David Rickman)

'In the name of God then, let us go forward.' The battle had begun. The time was about 3.45 a.m.

The original plan on coming up against the redoubts was that the two innermost columns would engage the line of forts, masking the fire to allow the outer two columns to pass through relatively unscathed. One of the problems was that many of the regimental and battalion commanders were unclear about their objectives: whether to storm the forts, bypass them or just harass them. The principal objective – the Russian camp – lay beyond the redoubt system

The first, incomplete, redoubt was stormed by the two battalions of the Dalcarian Regiment and those of the Västerbotten Regiment, while cavalry-

▼*Another portrayal of the Russian fortified camp, this time depicted after the Russian infantry have deployed in front of it. A number of heavy artillery pieces are shown lining the western rampart. The besieged town of Poltava is depicted in the background. (Painting by Martin the Younger, early eighteenth century; State Historical Museum, Moscow)*

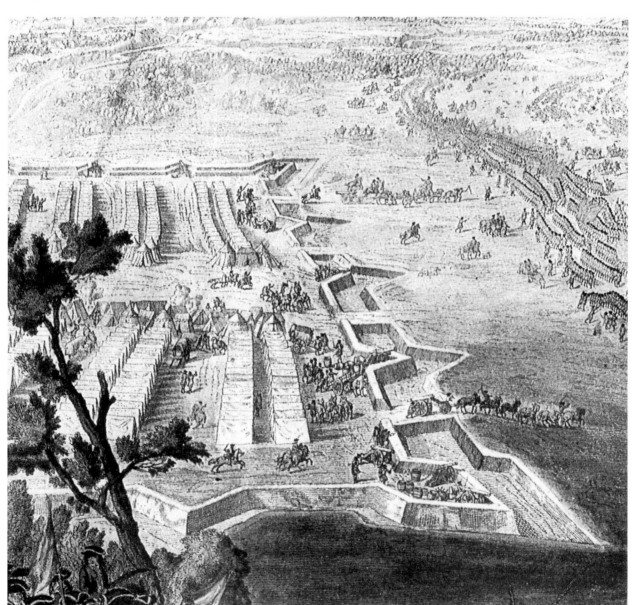

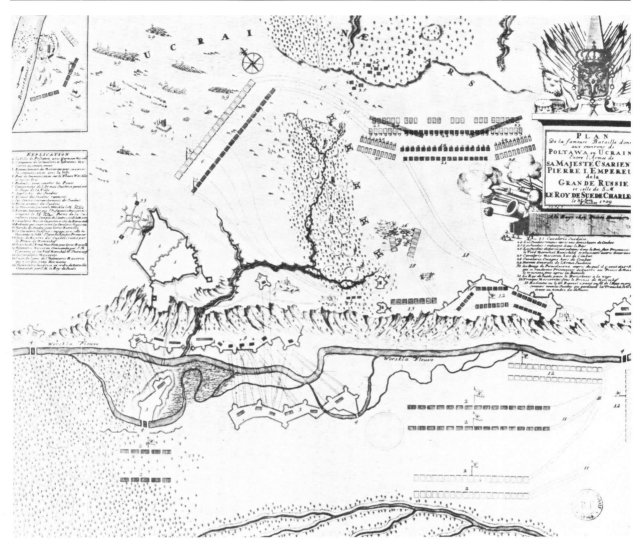

men of the Life Dragoon Regiment positioned themselves behind the fort, to hem the enemy in. The redoubt was taken rapidly, and all the defenders killed. By this the columns had become somewhat intermingled, the Guards battalions from Roos' column joining the fourth column, which was bypassing the redoubt line to the right. By this stage the Dalcarian Regiment had reached the second redoubt, which again was taken by storm, and the remaining defenders slaughtered.

While this was taking place, the columns to the left of the forts had advanced past the Dalcarians, but were drifting to the right in the early dawn gloom, arriving in front of the third redoubt. This was a larger fortification than the others, triangular in shape and defended by a full battalion with

▲ *Map of the battlefield of Poltava (28 June 1709). This rather inaccurate plan depicts several stages of the engagement, the Swedes starting from the upper left, facing the Russian redoubts. The final phase was fought in the centre-right, in front of the Russian fortified camp. Poltava and the Swedish siegeworks are shown on the left of the plan, the inset depicting the surrender of the Swedish army at Perovolochna. (Royal Armouries)*

artillery. The first battalion of the Narke-Varmland Regiment led the column, and launched itself directly at the redoubt. It was stopped in the ditch surrounding the fort, and the battalion recoiled in disorder into the Jönköping Regiment, which was coming up behind it. Both battalions reorganised

▼ *The Battle of Poltava (1709). This depiction of the early stages of the battle is highly inaccurate but shows Swedish infantry on the right of the picture amongst the line of Russian redoubts. A cavalry fight in the left of the painting represents the clash with Menshikov's blocking force* lined up behind the redoubt line. The town of Poltava is shown in the background. Note the omission of Yakovetski Wood. (Engraving by Larmessain after the original by Martin the Younger, early eighteenth century; State Historical Museum, Moscow)

and launched a second assault, which again was repulsed with heavy losses. While the battle continued around them, the third redoubt fought its own private war, as more Swedish battalions were sucked into the battle against the fortification.

On the right, the fourth column, which had been joined by three other battalions, was directly commanded by Lewenhaupt. As they neared the rear line of redoubts they saw that the bulk of Prince Menshikov's Russian horse was arrayed

The Battle of Poltava: Middle Stages

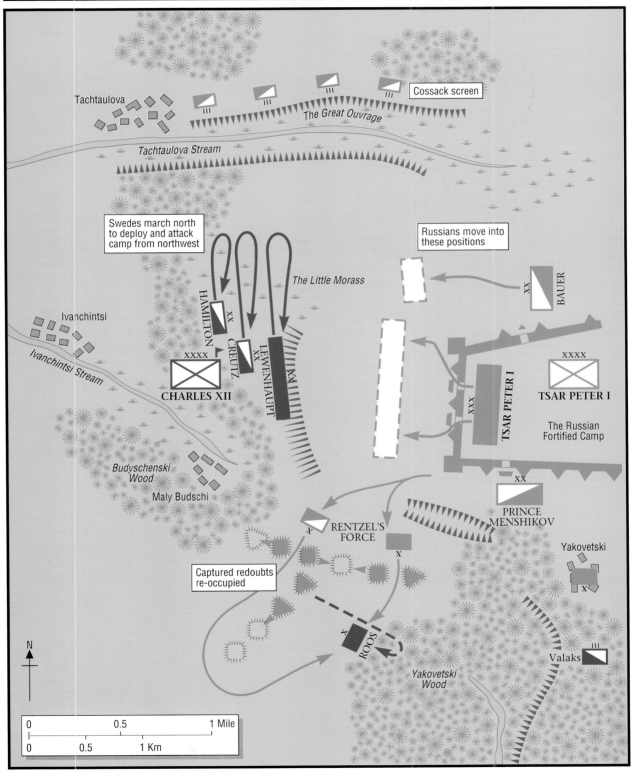

Tachtaulova

Cossack screen

The *Great Ouvrage*

Tachtaulova Stream

Swedes march north
to deploy and attack
camp from northwest

Russians move into
these positions

The *Little Morass*

BAUER

xx

Ivanchintsi

Ivanchintsi Stream

HAMILTON
xx

CREUTZ
xx

LEWENHAUPT

xxxx
CHARLES XII

TSAR PETER I

xxx

xxxx
TSAR PETER I

The Russian
Fortified Camp

Budyschenski
Wood

Maly Budschi

xx
PRINCE
MENSHIKOV

RENTZEL'S
FORCE
x

Yakovetski

x

Captured redoubts
re-occupied

x
ROOS

N

Yakovetski
Wood

Valaks
III

0		0.5		1 Mile
0	0.5		1 Km	

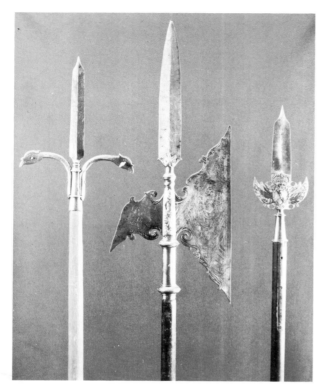

▲ *Russian artillery linstock and staff weapons of the reign of Tsar Peter I. Although the artillery linstock on the left is unadorned, both the sergeant's halberd and the officer's partisan (on the right) carry the monogram of the Tsar and the Russian military emblem of a crowned St. Andrew's cross. (State Museums of the Moscow Kremlin)*

behind them: 9,000 dragoons supported by horse artillery. As some of these horsemen moved through the redoubts towards the Swedish infantry, Lewenhaupt halted his men and called up cavalry support. The Swedish horse under General Creutz thundered past the right flank of the foot and turned west, towards the advancing Russians. More than 8,000 horsemen of both sides were now concentrated in the area between Lewenhaupt's infantry and the Russian redoubts. General Bauer, commanding the right wing of the Russian horse remained behind the rear line of redoubts to the west.

The initial two Swedish charges recoiled, and they pulled back to the east of the infantry line to regroup. Menshikov received orders from the Tsar to withdraw – orders he was unwilling to follow. By this stage the arena of the cavalry fight was obscured by columns of dust and smoke. A third Swedish charge finally forced the Russian dragoons to retire back through the redoubt line, and the pursuing Swedish horse were now forced to run a gauntlet of fire from the forts. Lewenhaupt ordered his infantry to follow up the cavalry, swinging his battalions to the right to avoid most of the fire from the redoubts.

On the Swedish left flank, General Hamilton led his horsemen through the western side of the rear line of redoubts, some of his men avoiding them completely by picking their way through Budyschenski Wood. Emerging on the far side, his lines were disordered, but the troopers were launched straight at the waiting Russian cavalry, who retreated after a brisk mêlée.

The Russian dragoons were now streaming away to the north, pursued by both wings of the Swedish horse. The time was about 4.30 in the morning.

Confusion during the passing of the projecting redoubt line meant that only the two battalions of the Västmanland Regiment remained on the Swedish left flank, and these followed in the wake of Hamilton's horsemen, storming one of the redoubts of the rear line on the way through. The rest of the Swedish foot were now either with Lewenhaupt on the right flank, who had just passed the line of redoubts, or still besieging the third redoubt in the projecting line. Unable to bypass the line completely, the Uppland Regiment under Lewenhaupt's immediate control stormed another redoubt of the rear line, which they took with heavy losses.

The Swedish infantry regrouped beyond the redoubts and took stock. Of the first column only the Västmanland Regiment could be found, out to the west of Lewenhaupt's position. The General now had ten battalions under his direct control: the second battalion of the Norke Värmland Regiment from the first column, the Östgöta and Uppland Regiments from the second column, the guardsmen from the third column and all of the fourth column, plus the supporting battery of artillery. The King was also with Lewenhaupt. Six battalions and General Roos were missing, presumably back behind the redoubts. This represented a third of the Swedish foot.

Lewenhaupt reformed his infantry and advanced towards the nearest corner of the Russian camp. He was stopped by a gully 100 metres from the fortification, and as his troops were manoeuvring to march around it he received the order from Rehnskold to call off the attack and regroup to the north-west. The Field Marshal considered an unsupported attack by part of the foot to be foolhardy, and planned to launch an attack once the cavalry and remaining infantry could be brought up in support.

The Swedish cavalry had pursued the Russian horse back towards the Great Ouvrage and the Tachtaulova stream when Rehnskold's order reached them to return and join Lewenhaupt's foot. While Menshikov had led some of the retreating Russian horse back into the fortified camp, the remainder now halted behind the Great Ouvrage, where General Bauer tried to restore order in their ranks. The time was now 5.30 a.m.

▶ *Detail of the final stages of the Battle of Poltava, with a cavalry fight in the foreground acting as the artistic scene-setter for the portrayal of the clash between the two infantry battle lines in the background. The village of Yakovetski is shown in the far distance, with the River Vorskla behind it. (Engraving by Larmessain after the original painting by Martin the Younger, early eighteenth century; State Historical Museum, Moscow)*

Lewenhaupt led his men into the low-lying ground in front of Budyschenski Wood, where they were joined by Rehnskold and the Swedish horse. The troops were shielded from the artillery fire of the Russian camp by the depression in the ground. There the army regrouped and waited for Roos and the remaining third of the infantry.

Roos and the Missing Battalions

Back at the third redoubt, the first battalion of the Narke-Värmland Regiment and the single battalion of the Jönsköping Regiment had been joined by the two small battalions of the Västerbotten Regiment. A further assault had just been repulsed, and the dead lay in heaps in the ditch surrounding the fort. At this point General Roos arrived from the south with the two battalions of the Dalcarian Regiment, following their successful storming of the second redoubt.

Colonel Siegroth, commanding the Dalcarians, led his men into the attack, but without ladders and siege equipment the troops were repulsed. Several more attacks were launched by the troops surrounding the redoubt over the next hour-and-a-half, as all six battalions struggled to take the fort. Casualties mounted without anything being achieved by the Swedes, and finally Roos decided to withdraw. Of the 2,600 men present in the six battalions at the start of the battle, more than 1,000 had been killed or seriously wounded. Roos withdrew his small force to the east, reforming beyond range of the redoubt guns, at the edge of Yakovetski Wood. It was now 6.00 a.m., and he had no idea where the rest of the army was.

▼ *Early eighteenth-century Swedish cavalry deployed for the attack. The squadron is arrayed in three ranks but has not yet formed into its chevron formation. The cavalry are shown riding boot-to-boot. When in their chevron, the ranks would be boot-behind-boot, with the formation centred around the cornet shown here accompanying the officer in the centre of the front rank. The staff officer facing away from the viewer may represent Field Marshal Rehnskold. (Drawing by an unknown German artist, early eighteenth century; Royal Armouries)*

Russian cavalry. Left to right: Troopers of the Inger-manlandski Dragoon Regiment and Kropotov's Horse Grenadier Regiment; and a Drummer of the Inger-manlandski Regiment, with that regiment's flag in the background. (Painting by David Rickman)

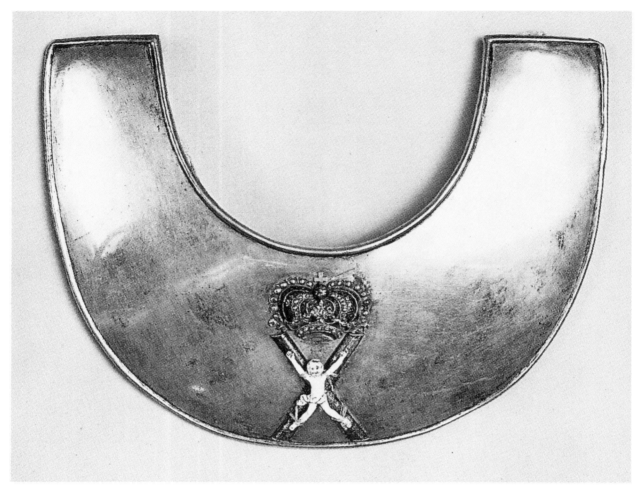

▲ *Russian officer's gorget, c. 1706–20. One of several variants, the decoration is painted on to the brass surface. It was suspended from the neck by means of crimson ribbons. This example is reputed to have belonged to Tsar Peter I. (State Artillery Museum, St. Petersburg)*

As Roos reformed his troops and the main Swedish army waited for news of his force, the Russians took the initiative. Learning that a third of the Swedish foot was isolated, a force was despatched to attack it. While the captured redoubts were re-occupied by Russian troops, Lieutenant General Rentzel emerged from the Russian camp with five battalions of infantry to attack Roos. He was supported by a column of five dragoon regiments commanded by Lieutenant General Heinske, who swept around the line of redoubts to attack Roos from the south-west. Caught between the two forces, Roos deployed his battalions in a curve, his back to the wood, with one battalion amongst the trees to prevent outflanking by the Russian foot. The Swedish battalions had not completed their reorganisation after the attack on the redoubt, and heavy officer casualties meant that control was difficult. During a brief fire-fight the Swedes began to fall back in the face of the Russian infantry, who then fell on with bayonets and pikes.

The Swedish line broke under the assault. A Swedish sergeant-major recalled, 'All was in vain as the pike points of the enemy were at us to the body, so the majority were wounded to death by them.'

The Dalcarlian Regiment screened the Russian dragoons long enough for the survivors to flee, the majority escaping down a ravine into the interior of the wood. More than 1,100 Swedes were killed or captured, as Roos led the remainder along the ravine to the south-east, fighting off the Russians who surrounded his band. He planned to lead his men to the comparative safety of the Poltava siege

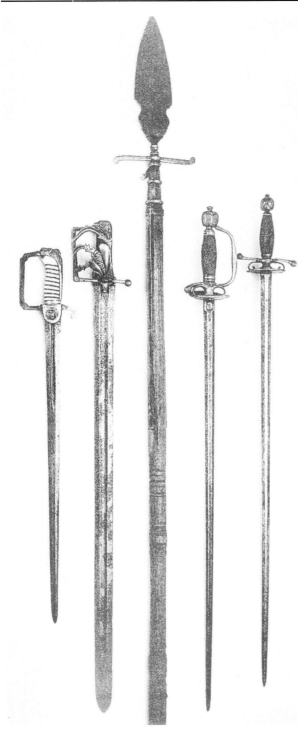

◀ *These edged weapons form part of a case in the State Historical Museum, Moscow, bearing the caption: 'Side-arms of Russian army officers, early eighteenth century'. Although the spontoon or partisan is probably mid-eighteenth century, the swords are more probably Petrine; the left two being a naval hanger and a cavalry broad-sword (back-sword) respectively, while both the examples on the right are infantry officer's small-swords.*

metres south-east of the cloisters, overlooking the Vorskla. It was 9.00 a.m. Roos was now besieged in the redoubt, and as the Russians brought up regimental artillery and fresh troops he prepared the fortification for the expected assault. When Rentzel, the Russian commander, offered Roos the opportunity to surrender he requested time to consider the proposal. Consulting his officers and men, he reached the conclusion that further resistance was indeed futile – 'the soldiers had shot all away'. Recalling Rentzel, the Swedish general surrendered his force, and his men were marched northwards to the Russian fortified camp. The Swedes had lost a third of their infantry before the main battle had even started.

The Swedish Attack

As the morning continued to pass with no sign of movement on the part of the main Swedish army, the Tsar decided to regain the initiative. News had reached him that Roos and the remnants of his command were fleeing towards the cloisters south of Yakovetski Wood and could no longer influence the outcome of the battle. Three extra battalions were sent to assist Rentzel in securing the surrender of that force. It was now 8.45 a.m. As Peter held a council of war, the Swedes were seen to move off to the north, apparently attempting to come between the camp and the remaining Russian cavalry north of the Great Ouvrage. If the Russian horse could be held at bay, then an attack on the north-western corner of the fortified camp would cut the Russians off from their line of retreat. Superiority in numbers would be negated by the lack of room to manoeuvre within the camp, and the trapped infantry could be decimated by a spirited Swedish assault, as had happened at Narva.

lines, but, on emerging from the wood by the cloisters, he found the way blocked by fresh Russian infantry – four battalions from the Poltava garrison.

All other options denied him, Roos led his by now exhausted troops to an abandoned redoubt 500

Weather: very hot, sunshine obscured by smoke from Russian guns

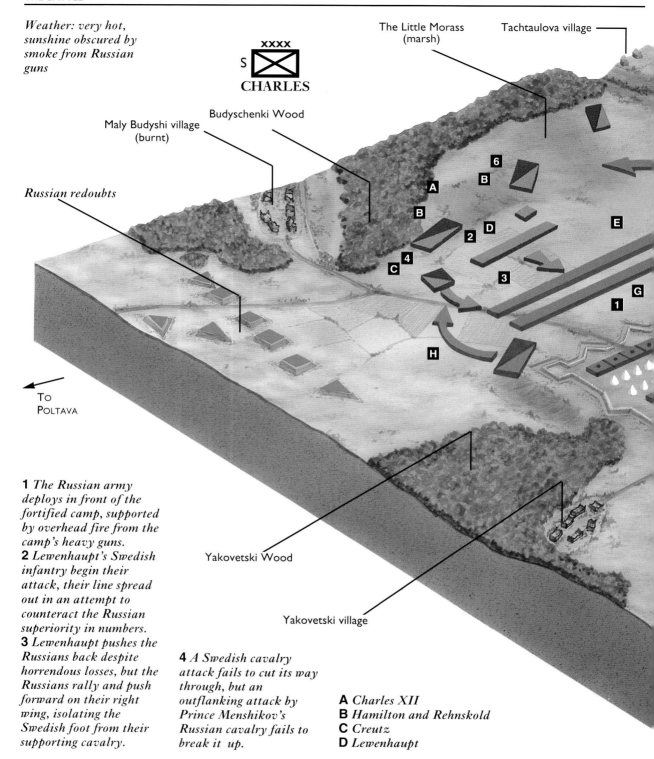

The Little Morass (marsh)

Tachtaulova village

S **CHARLES**

Budyschenki Wood

Maly Budyshi village (burnt)

Russian redoubts

To POLTAVA

Yakovetski Wood

Yakovetski village

1 *The Russian army deploys in front of the fortified camp, supported by overhead fire from the camp's heavy guns.*
2 *Lewenhaupt's Swedish infantry begin their attack, their line spread out in an attempt to counteract the Russian superiority in numbers.*
3 *Lewenhaupt pushes the Russians back despite horrendous losses, but the Russians rally and push forward on their right wing, isolating the Swedish foot from their supporting cavalry.*

4 *A Swedish cavalry attack fails to cut its way through, but an outflanking attack by Prince Menshikov's Russian cavalry fails to break it up.*

A *Charles XII*
B *Hamilton and Rehnskold*
C *Creutz*
D *Lewenhaupt*

THE BATTLE OF POLTAVA

The Swedish final attack, about noon, 28 June 1709, as seen from the south-east

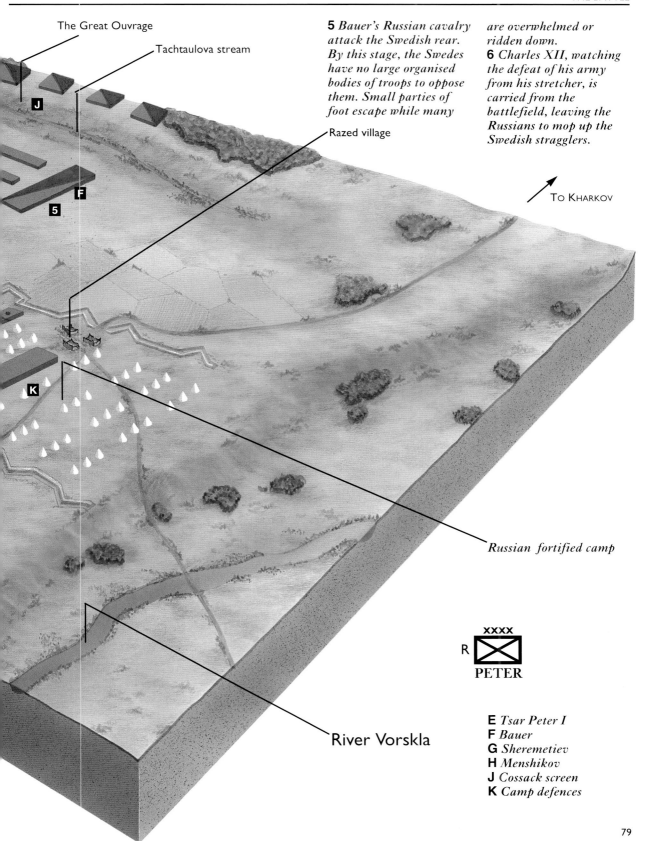

The Great Ouvrage

Tachtaulova stream

J

F

5

Razed village

K

5 *Bauer's Russian cavalry attack the Swedish rear. By this stage, the Swedes have no large organised bodies of troops to oppose them. Small parties of foot escape while many*

are overwhelmed or ridden down.
6 *Charles XII, watching the defeat of his army from his stretcher, is carried from the battlefield, leaving the Russians to mop up the Swedish stragglers.*

TO KHARKOV

Russian fortified camp

River Vorskla

xxxx

R ⊠ PETER

E *Tsar Peter I*
F *Bauer*
G *Sheremetiev*
H *Menshikov*
J *Cossack screen*
K *Camp defences*

◀ *The Battle of Poltava (1709). The Tsar, escorted by a dragoon regiment, is shown in the foreground on a hill that reflects contemporary artistic convention rather than battlefield topography. The Russian fortified camp is depicted in the background. (Engraving by Larmessain, after 1725; State Hermitage Museum, St. Petersburg)*

▶ *The Battle of Poltava (1709). Russian dragoons are shown with Tsar Peter I at their head. In reality the Tsar stationed himself with the Preobrazhenski Guard on the right of the Russian line during the final stages of the battle. Engraving by Larmessain after the painting by Martin the Younger, early eighteenth century. (State Historical Museum, Moscow).*

Peter ordered his troops to deploy in the open ground in front of the camp, and his foot began to file out and to re-form outside. The manoeuvre was completed within half an hour, the infantry arrayed in two ranks, the first of 24 battalions, the second of 18. In all, the Russian infantry lines comprised 22,000 men, all facing to the west.

The whole battle line covered a 2,000-metre frontage. Regimental guns were brought into position in the intervals between the regiments, 55 pieces in all. The larger pieces of artillery remained in the camp, where their elevated position allowed them to fire over the heads of their own infantry. Nine battalions of infantry remained in the camp to protect the guns and to act as a general reserve.

Bauer's horse deployed to the right of the infantry, 9,000 dragoons in 11 regiments. Prince Menshikov brought 4,800 dragoons in 6 regiments round behind the left wing of the infantry, deploying with his flank resting on Yakovetski Wood. The remainder of the Russian cavalry – Hetman Skoropadski's Cossacks – remained north of the Great Ouvrage.

Both Charles XII and Rehnskold saw the danger they were now in. Their move north had placed them at risk of being cut off from their baggage train to the south, and there was a real danger of the

small Swedish army being boxed in if the main Russian line swung north. Charles ordered an immediate march south, and the army retraced its steps to the low ground where it had spent the early part of the morning. Hamilton's cavalry remained on the left flank of the infantry, but Creutz's horse found they lacked the room to deploy because of the line of redoubts to the south, so they formed up behind Lewenhaupt's infantry. The Swedish infantry battalions were spaced out to increase their frontage, but at 1,500 metres the line was outflanked by the Russians. Ten battalions were deployed in four ranks, with the two battalions of the Västmanland Regiment drawn up behind the left flank of the infantry line.

The Tsar, mounted on his horse Finette, rode up and down the line as Orthodox priests sprinkled holy water. The Russian line then started to advance, closing the gap between the two armies. The time was now 9.45 a.m. If the Swedes remained where they were they would be pinned with their backs to Budyschenski Wood and overwhelmed. The only option now was to attack. Rehnskold ordered Lewenhaupt to advance. With the words, 'Then, in the name of Jesus, may God stand mercifully by us', Lewenhaupt gave the command and the Swedish line moved forward.

From contemporary accounts, it appears that the two armies lay approximately 800 metres apart, so at the regulated speed of an approach march the Swedes would take almost ten minutes to reach the waiting Russians. From the outset the heavy Russian guns fired shot over the heads of their own troops from their elevated position in the Russian fortified camp. This fire had an effect more psychological than any other at that range. But after approximately 3 minutes the Swedes came within range of the 77 regimental guns ranged along the front of the Russian line. The combined bombardment began to have an effect, cutting down whole files of the attackers. Smoke rolled from the Russian line towards the Swedes, partly obscuring the combatants and making orientation difficult. When the Swedish infantry had advanced to within 200 metres of the defenders, the artillerymen switched to canister fire. The effect of this was likened to 'a hailstorm', scything down men in whole ranks – in the words of a surviving officer, 'mown down by the thunderous Russian cannon before they could find employment for their muskets'. (Von Weihe, quoted in Englund 1992)

At this point the advancing line began to lose cohesion. It is unknown whether the two battalions on the Swedish left were checked for a moment

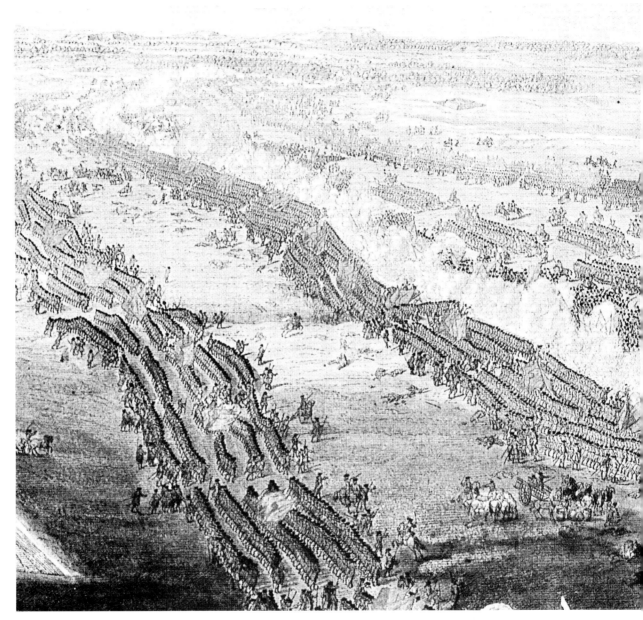

before continuing, but they had begun to lag behind the main line and drift slightly away from it, towards their left.

When the Swedish line reached a position 40 metres from them, the front line of Russian infantry opened up with a volley of musket fire. Lewenhaupt wrote later that 'it were impossible humanly to believe that any man at all of our sorely pressed infantry could emerge from it with his life'. The rapidly thinning Swedish ranks still continued to advance, leaving a band of dead and wounded lying behind them on the steppe. The survivors then halted, according to training, fired a volley into the Russian ranks and charged. Several units of the first Russian line began to waver, then retired in some disorder. For a moment it looked as if the Swedish attack would live up to the unbelievably high hopes held of it. The Russians were in danger of having their front line pinned between their second line and the Swedish bayonets. Contact was made on the Swedish right and centre.

◀ *Detail of an engraving of the Battle of Poltava (1709) by Larmessain. The Russian regiments on the left of the picture are shown deployed into two lines, the battalions interspersed by regimental guns. The attacking battalions of Lewenhaupt's Swedish infantry are shown advancing from the right of the picture. (State Hermitage Museum, St. Petersburg)*

be outflanked, then surrounded if they were unable to break the Russian centre. Their situation was roughly similar to that facing the Romans at the battle of Cannae (216 BC). The major difference was the lack of cohesion in the Swedish line. As the Swedish battalions had been widely separated to help meet the Russian frontage, there were large spaces in the Swedish frontage. This was accentuated by the increasing gap between the battalions on the left wing and the main Swedish line.

The Swedish drive had left three Russian regiments unengaged on the Russian left flank, and these now became the target for attack by the Swedish horse on the Swedish right flank, commanded by Creutz. The cavalry had been disorganised in the manoeuvring before the Swedish attack, and only a portion of the troopers present were available to charge in support of the foot. On approaching the Russian line they discovered that two of the Russian regiments (Nizhni-Novgorodski and Busch's Grenadiers) had formed a brigade-sized square, supported by regimental artillery. The charge failed to break the square, and the Swedish horse recoiled in disorder.

Although the impetus of the attack by the Swedish right was carrying it forwards, the rest of the line was making no headway and was heavily outnumbered. The strongest part of the Russian first infantry line was its right wing, consisting of two veteran infantry regiments and the Semenovski and Preobrazhenski Guard Regiments, commanded by General Golitsyn. These began to press forward, pushing back the Swedish left wing. The Narke-Värmland and Östgöta units were now facing an oncoming wave of Russian battalions, and both units broke, the men fleeing to the rear. This exposed the left flank of the two-battalion Uppland Regiment, and the four regiments of Golitsyn's command flooded into the breach. The Russian Narvski and Schlusselburgski Regiments advanced into the gap

While the Swedish right wing pushed back the Russians, who were now to some extent hampered by their own numbers, on the left wing the attackers faced the Russian Guards regiments, who outflanked the Swedes of the Narke-Varmland and Ostgota Regiments. Contact was delayed by the lagging Swedish battalions, so the centre and right were carving their way deeper into the Russian line before the left wing had reached the enemy. The real danger of the Swedish position was that their infantry were overlapped on both sides, and inevitably would

◀ *Ceremonial entry of Russian troops into Moscow after their victory at Poltava on 21 December 1709. Dragoon escort detachments in the foreground follow the Tsar and his senior officers, who in turn follow a line of Swedish prisoners and a selection of all arms of the Russian army. Church bells were rung for an entire week and tables covered with food and beer were placed in the streets, while cannon were fired from the walls of the Kremlin in celebration. (Engraving by A. Zubov, 1711; State Historical Museum, St. Petersburg)*

created between the Upplanders and the Swedish left wing, irrevocably breaking the last semblance of a Swedish line.

Lewenhaupt tried to rally his left wing without success. Major General Sparre, after trying to rally troops fleeing past his supporting Västmänland Regiment said to Lewenhaupt, 'The Devil couldn't make them stand.' As the Swedish cavalry on the left wing were either facing superior numbers of Russian horse or were disordered, there was nothing Lewenhaupt could do to save the situation. His infantry had now been surrounded, and were being ground down by superior numbers. Rather than resort to hand-to-hand combat, the Russians preferred to use firepower to finish off the enemy foot. The battle had become a slaughter. It was not yet 11.00 a.m.

Menshikov led his six dragoon regiments southwest of the infantry battle, then looped back north, deploying into line in the vicinity of the eastern end of the line of redoubts. His dragoons then advanced into the rear of Creutz's Swedish horse, which were still facing the square of Russian foot. The Swedes recovered and forced Menshikov to withdraw, but by this stage the disorder spreading through the rest of the army had reached the cavalry, and no further concerted moves were possible. A number of individual Swedish cavalry units launched uncoordi-

nated attacks on the Russian foot engulfing Lewenhaupt's battalions, some with a degree of temporary success. The Russian square still remained immobile because of the continued threat of a cavalry charge. This enabled the two guard battalions on the right of the Swedish line to retire in some semblance of order.

The disordered state of the Swedish cavalry at the start of the attack was largely due to their deployment between the infantry and Budyschenski Wood before the attack began. Apart from a small portion commanded by Creutz, they failed to order their ranks and deploy before the infantry were engaged. This meant that at the vital stage when the momentum of Lewenhaupt's attack carried the line forward, their support was unavailable. Pressure of encirclement from the Russian dragoons to the north of the battle arena increased as the infantry fight began, and when General Bauer ordered his Russian horse forward, the Swedes had few organised bodies with which to stop them. Bauer's advance was contained for a time by counter-charges from the Skane Dragoon Regiment and the Östgöta Cavalry Regiment, who, by holding off repeated Russian attacks allowed the remainder of the unengulfed Swedish army to escape from the battlefield.

Charles XII saw little of the final stages of the battle, his viewpoint obscured by smoke. He had

▶ *The silver medal awarded to participants in the Battle of Poltava, issued in 1709. It carries a portrait of the Tsar on the obverse, while the reverse depicts a stylised clash between cavalry and infantry from both sides, with the town of Poltava in the background. (State Historical Museum, St. Petersburg)*

remained behind when the infantry attack was launched, and his fears were confirmed when Rehnskold reported that the foot were running away. The battle had been lost.

Pursuit and Surrender

The Swedish infantry battalions that had formed the main line had for the most part been slaughtered, their locations marked by mounds of bodies. The two battalions on either end of the line had managed to escape with at least a core of their original number, but only a handful escaped from the remaining battalions. Of the cavalry, those who had not been squandered in charges to hold off the enemy dragoons or in trying to rescue the infantry were now fleeing the field. The four field pieces were abandoned.

The main line of retreat south was blocked by the line of redoubts, still garrisoned by Russian troops. With enemy on all three other sides, the only means of escape was through Budyschenski Wood and the marshes surrounding Ivanchintsi stream. As the Swedes fled westwards, Tsar Peter's cavalry pursued them, supported by roving bands of Cossacks. Horses and men floundered in the marsh as artillery fire continued to be directed on the fleeing Swedes. By the time he had crossed the stream, King Charles had lost 21 of the original 24 guardsmen detailed to carry and protect his stretcher. Acting as the focal point for a growing number of troops, his party then headed south towards Pushkaryovka and the baggage train.

Substantial Swedish casualties were sustained during the pursuit, and while the Russian infantry halted at the stream, bands of Cossacks and dragoons continued to harry the fugitives as far as Pushkaryovka, picking off stragglers and small isolated units. During this stage Field Marshal Rehnskold and Chancellor Piper were captured, both while attempting to stem the rout. Meanwhile, following the surrender of Roos, the Swedish battalions manning the siegeworks around Poltava had come under increasing pressure from the garrison, although they held their positions until recalled to Pushkaryovka by the King.

While his soldiers patched their wounds and counted their dead, the Tsar held a victory mass and banquet on the battlefield, inviting Rehnskold and other captured Swedish senior officers. At the banquet, when Peter proposed a toast to 'my teachers' (the Swedes), Rehnskold replied that 'the pupils have delivered a good return to their masters'. This lesson had been taught at significant expense; the Swedes had lost some 6,900 men on the battlefield that morning, with a further 2,800 being taken prisoner. This represented just over half their army, and many of the survivors were wounded. An even more important casualty was the self-esteem of the army. The Swedish army was a machine that expected victory. In defeat, the machine began to fall apart.

Russian losses have been estimated as being 1,345 killed and around 3,200 wounded. Given the appallingly inadequate medical provision in both armies, any seriously wounded soldier had little chance of survival.

Charles XII led the remnants of his army south during the night, gathering up his outposts along the Vorskla as he went. Retreat towards Poland was impractical. His options were reduced to marching on the Turkish border at Ochakov, or heading over the steppe to the Crimea, from where his army could hope to be shipped to safety by the Ottomans. The former option was the more preferable, although it meant forcing a crossing of the Dniepr, so an advanced guard was sent ahead to secure a rumoured crossing site and to build ferries. The number of wagons was reduced to two per regiment, and the army continued south, following the banks of the Vorskla while fighting off Cossack raids as it marched. During the afternoon of 30 June, the main Swedish army caught up with their vanguard on the banks of the Dniepr at Perovolochna.

The truth then dawned on the King: there were few boats and no bridge waiting for his troops, and the barren nature of the countryside meant that there was insufficient timber to build anything. The battered army was now gathered on the banks of an impassable river in an area of low-lying marshes and fields, overlooked by sandhills – a natural trap. Hopes were pinned on the Russians being unable to organise a pursuing force in time to catch the Swedes, and plans were drawn up somehow to ferry the army across the Vorskla and march towards the Crimea. The Cossacks accompanying the army were ordered to swim the Dniepr, which was undertaken with numerous losses, as men and horses were swept away.

A mood of terrible fatalism had descended on the Swedish troops. Morale and discipline began to break down. Crowds flocked to the river bank as men attempted to cross by whatever means were available. It was obvious to everyone that the army was in little position to fight if the Russians caught

up with them. During the evening the King was persuaded to cross the river to safety, accompanied by over 300 Drabants, foot escort, staff officers and his personal entourage. One account cited by Englund reports that no boats were available for other troops as 'more than were needed by the great and noble lords, who filled the places on the crossing'. General Lewenhaupt was left in command of the dying army, with orders to march on the Crimea. Plans were drawn up and attempts were made to try to bring some order to the chaotic mess by the riverside.

As dawn broke on 1 July, Lewenhaupt was made aware of enemy activity to his north. Creutz was sent to investigate, only to discover a small Russian all-arms force deployed and ready to attack. Any hope of escape was now out of the question. The Russian troops were a flying corps (*korvolan*) of 9,000 men; the Preobrazhenski and Semenovski Guard Regiments, 8 dragoon regiments and two batteries of horse artillery. The force, commanded by Prince Menshikov, had been able to catch up with the Swedes by mounting the infantry two to a horse, so allowing them to keep up with the dragoons.

A wave of panic swept the Swedish troops, and crowds milled around the river bank. Lewenhaupt drew what he could of his army into a battle line behind a marsh at the foot of the sand hills and considered his next move. He sought the opinion of his officers, but received no clear support for either surrender or a final fight. Messengers flitted between the two commands until by 11 a.m., Lewenhaupt had made up his mind: the Swedish Royal Army would surrender. While the Swedes would be treated fairly, it was deemed that all rebel Cossacks should be 'delivered up to His Tsarist Majesty'. This meant immediate execution. So, on 1 July 1709, at Perovolochna in the Ukraine, 20,000 Swedish soldiers, their families, servants and artisans were marched into captivity. The total included 9,152 horsemen, 3,286 infantrymen, 137 gunners and 983 officers, the remainder being non-combatants. The majority of these would be released after the signing of the Treaty of Nystadt, in 1721.

Meanwhile, the King and his escort escaped to the Turkish border.

Although an anachronism in the rest of Europe, pikes were still used extensively by both the Swedish and Russian armies. Swedish battalions generally deployed with pikes in the centre and two equal wings of musketeers. (Painting by David Rickman)

AFTERMATH

Poltava must certainly rate as one of Europe's most significant battles. It marked a turning-point in the fortunes of two empires – the start of the decline of the sixty-year Swedish empire; and the rise of Russia as a European power.

The Great Northern War was to drag on for another twelve years, but after 1709 Sweden was isolated and on the strategic defensive. Within a year both Saxony-Poland and Denmark would rejoin the anti-Swedish cause, and the capture of Vyborg to the north of St. Petersburg and Riga to the south would ensure the safety of Tsar Peter's fledgling European capital. In Peter's view, this was the greatest achievement of the battle. In a report of the action he added that 'with God's help the last foundation stone of St. Petersburg has been laid'. Over the next six years the anti-Swedish alliance continued to cut away Sweden's overseas possessions: first the Baltic States, then Finland. Sensing blood, Prussia and Hannover joined the alliance in 1715 so that they could divide up Sweden's territories in Germany. Despite the attempts of Charles XII to force Turkey into war with Russia, the Swedish demise continued. When a Turkish war was forced upon him in 1711, Peter escaped disaster when his army was surrounded by bargaining his way out.

Charles himself remained a virtual prisoner in Turkey until 1714 when he escaped, arriving back in time to participate in the Swedish surrender of Stralsund, her last remaining foothold outside her homeland. Refusing to accept peace negotiations, the Swedish monarch continued to fight on, protecting the Swedish homeland until he was killed during a siege in southern Norway in 1718. His country was by now drained of manpower and financially destitute, and Russian amphibious raids were devastating her coastline. By this stage, Russia's allies had made peace, having won their share of the prize and by now jealous of the rising power of the Russian state. Russia continued the war alone, until in 1721 the Swedish government had no option but to sue for peace.

Englund summed up the effects of the conflict from the Swedish perspective: 'When the long-delayed peace was finally concluded it signalled the end of the Swedish imperium. At the same time – more importantly – it confirmed the birth of a new great European power – Russia. This realm was to grow ever greater and more mighty; an empire in the lee of which the Swedes would have to learn to live. In terms of world history, the people of an entire nation had left the stage and taken their seat among the spectators.' (Englund 1992).

CHRONOLOGY

Events leading to the Battle of Poltava:

27 August 1707 The Swedish army leaves Altranstadt in Saxony.

28 January 1708 Grodno entered by Swedes.

March Swedish army encamps at Radoshkoviche in Lithuania.

3 July Battle of Holowczyn. Russians defeated.

7 July Moghilev entered by Swedes.

31 August Small battle at Malatitze (Dobroe). Russian attack repulsed.

4 September Tatarsk entered by Swedes. Nearest Swedes will come to Moscow.

15 September Charles XII orders Swedish army to march south into Severia.

28 September Battle of Lesnaya. Swedes under Lewenhaupt defeated

8 October Charles XII and Lewenhaupt join forces. Swedes march on Ukraine.

2 November Menshikov crushes Ukrainian Cossack revolt and burns Baturin.

December Armies enter winter quarters.

7 January 1709 Assault on Veprik. Costly success for Swedes.

1 May Siege of Poltava commences.

16 June Russian army crosses Vorskla.

27 June Swedes prepare to launch attack.

28 June: The Battle of Poltava

3.45 Swedes launch attack.

4.00 Passage of the redoubts. Storming of the first two redoubts.

4.20 Cavalry battle begins around redoubts.

4.40 Russian cavalry retreat northwards

5.00 Lewenhaupt prepares to attack camp. Roos attacks third redoubt.

5.30 Swedes regroup in low-lying ground.

6.00 Roos regroups to east of redoubt.

6.15 Roos attacked by Russian foot and horse. His force broken. Retreat to Poltava.

8.30 Swedish army moves north.

9.00 Russian army deploys outside camp.

9.30 Roos surrenders his surviving command.

9.45 Swedish infantry launch attack.

10.10 Russian right wing advances. Menshikov attacks Creutz's cavalry.

10.30 Swedish left wing breaks. Bauer advances with Russian cavalry.

10.45 Swedish infantry line overrun. General rout of Swedish troops.

11.00 Charles XII leaves the battlefield.

12.00 Russian infantry recalled from pursuit.

Events following the Battle of Poltava

28 June 1709 Charles XII gathers troops around baggage train and retreats south.

29 June Troops sent ahead to secure crossings over the Dniepr.

30 June Dniepr reached, but no means of crossing available. King escapes with entourage.

31 June Menshikov catches up with Swedish army at Perovolochka. Swedish army surrenders.

◀ *Augustus II, Elector of Saxony and King of Poland. His abdication and peace treaty with the Swedes freed Charles XII to plan for his attack on Russia. After Poltava he was reinstated as king of Poland with the support of Tsar Peter, and henceforth would always conduct his policies under the shadow of his mentor. (Royal Armouries)*

A GUIDE TO FURTHER READING

There is little published on the campaign in English. I have listed only sources that are readily available in this language. A list of available Russian and Swedish source material is given in the more extensive bibliographies of Duffy (for the Russian sources) and Englund and Hatton (for the Swedes). Amongst these of particular relevance are the works of Beskrovnyi, Shotiv, Tengberg and the Swedish General Staff.

Chandler, D. *The Art of Warfare in the Age of Marlborough*, London, 1976. Excellent description of the nuts and bolts of the early eighteenth century military machine as used in Europe.

Duffy, C. *Russia's Military Way to the West*, London, 1981. Detailed study of the eighteenth-century Russian army and a summary of its campaigns.

Englund, P. *The Battle of Poltava*, London, 1992. A bestseller in Sweden, this provides a detailed Swedish perspective to the battle. Recommended.

Hatton, R. M. *Charles XII of Sweden*, London, 1968. Dr. Hatton's scholarly biography is still unsurpassed, replacing earlier romantic portrayals.

— *Captain Jefferye's letters from the Swedish army, 1707–9*, Stockholm, 1954. Diary of the only English observer in the Swedish army. Valuable background material.

Jackson, W. G. F. *Seven Roads to Moscow*, London, 1957. Overview of several invasions of Russia, including that of 1708–9. Now rather dated.

Konstam, A. *The Army of Peter the Great*, (2 volumes), London, 1993. First substantial English work on Tsar Peter's army, including organisation and uniforms.

Massie, R. K. *Peter the Great*, London, 1981 The definitive English-language biography of the Tsar. Recommended.

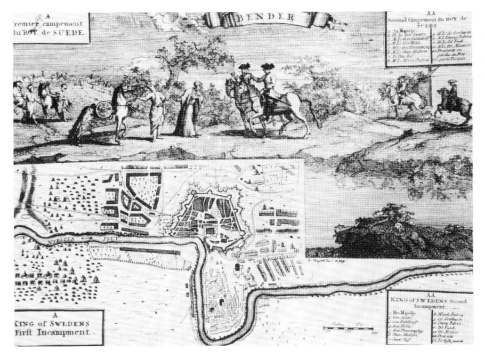

◀ *The Swedish camp at Bender, in Turkey, 1711. When Charles XII was granted asylum for himself and his followers, an encampment was built to the south of the Turkish town of Bender (the area in the bend of the River Dniestr). The upper portion of the print depicts the King riding in the countryside, accompanied by Major General Axel Sparre. (Author's collection)*

THE BATTLEFIELD TODAY

In 1709, the town of Poltava was already spreading beyond its walls. Today, modern industrial and residential suburbs surround the old town on all sides, including east of the Vorskla. The villages of Ribtsi and Pushkaryovka are still outside the city. Much of the marshland along the Vorskla has been drained, the land now being used for farming. Traces of both Budyschenski and Yakovetski Woods still remain, the latter bisected by the railway line running from Kiev to Poltava. A further railway crosses the Vorskla by a bridge that runs through the location of the redoubt where Roos surrendered.

The location of the main battlefield is crossed by a modern road, running roughly from the line of redoubts, through the fortified camp and off to the north. The area is used for farming, and a number of buildings cover the battlefield. Around the site of the eastern end of the redoubt line is a large mound, known as 'Mogila Shvedskii' (the Swedish Grave); despite popular legend, this contains the bodies of the *Russian* dead, the Swedes having been buried where they fell. A large monument to the victory stands by the roadside.

The Poltava museum contains displays relating to the battle, including a diorama. All trophies were removed to Moscow or St. Petersburg, where they may be viewed in the relevant museum collections (the State Historic Museum, Moscow, the State Artillery Museum and the Hermitage Museum, St. Petersburg).

WARGAMING THE POLTAVA CAMPAIGN

The Great Northern War (1700–21) has been a period neglected by wargamers until quite recently. Wargamers propping up the bar will speak about 'periods', enthusing about 'Ancients', 'Napoleonics', or (more rarely) 'Marlburian' periods. By the latter the wargamer usually means the War of the Spanish Succession, fought between France (and allies) and the maritime powers (and allies). This 'Corporal John' enthusiast will have heard of Peter the Great, most probably have read that Charles XII was a +3 on all die rolls general, and would have a vague idea that Poltava was an important battle. The Great Northern war represents the great unexplored 'period' – a potential wargaming epic of *War and Peace* proportions.

At various times the war involved Sweden, Russia, Norway, Denmark, Saxony, Poland, Brandenburg-Prussia, Hannover, England and the Netherlands. It saw the decline of Sweden as a great power, eclipsed by Russia as the dominant force on the east European stage. In other words, it was no side-show, or warm-up act for 'Corporal John'! Instead of the 'Marlburian' period, wargamers should really refer to it as the 'Petrine' or 'Carolean' period!

In the last few years wargamers have shown signs that things are changing. To my knowledge at least six manufacturers produce figures for the war, rules now take account of the conflict and related articles now appear in the wargames press. What follows are a few suggestions that allow these new wargaming resources to be used, breathing life into the 'period'.

Skirmish Level Games

Several rule sets are available. One in particular, *Once upon a time in the West Country* (from Partisan Press) lends itself well to the period, although the rules themselves are designed for the English Civil War. They allow the use of pikemen and, being simple, can readily be adapted to the period. Other sets are available, but anything that allows the control of individual figure bases with up to fifty figures a side would be adequate. A number of suggested scenarios could be as follows.

Russian Cossacks harassing a Swedish foraging party. By keeping the enemy in the saddle by continual alarms, the Cossacks were able to reduce the fighting potential of the Swedish army. An account in Peter Englund's *Poltava* mentions a Cossack raid during a church service on the eve of Poltava. He also records that when Swedish ambushes were laid, poor quality of powder prevented the Swedes inflicting serious casualties on their adversaries. Both the exhaustion of the Swedes and their poor powder quality could be factored into the scenario.

Charles XII was wounded when inspecting his outposts along the River Vorskla. Another scenario could be 'shoot the VIP', where Cossack marksmen on the far side of the river try to wing either the King or one of his accompanying generals. Remember that the range of a Cossack rifled musket was far greater than that of a Swedish musket.

A case of mistaken identity. Both Rehnskold and Piper were captured after Poltava when they rode back to the battlefield to try to salvage something from the defeat. You could have one of these two accompanied by a small escort or staff riding up to a unit, discovering they were Russian dragoons and trying to get away. This would be a bit like the Pony Express trying to evade the pursuing Apaches, as seen in countless westerns!

When the retreating Swedish army reached the River Dnieper at Perovolochka they found nothing with which to cross the river. As discipline broke down, anything that could float became worth its weight in gold. The scene would be set for a struggle between groups of Swedes over a raft that one group had made. This would involve fighting with clubbed muskets, spades and fists – an eighteenth century gang fight.

After Poltava (or for that matter any of the battles) small groups of the losing side made their way to the rear, hoping to join larger units and eventually to link up with the remains of their army. A group of Swedes could try to pick their way across the table while various enemy groups could appear from one or more table edges in an attempt to stop them. Think of the retreat from Moscow and you get the idea.

Battalion-Level Games

A recent wargaming development has been the introduction of battalion-level games, where a stand represents a company or sub-unit of one, using a figure scale of one figure equals ten men. As far as I know, the only ones available are again from Partisan Press. *File Leader* for the English Civil War or *Ranger* for the French and Indian Wars could be adapted. To my mind this is an extremely satisfying level at which to fight a game. An army of a handful of battalions and a smattering of officers on individual stands offers the flexibility with which to fight a number of the smaller actions of the campaign. The rules covering 'officer incidents' certainly liven up the game; for example, take this extract from *File Leader*:

Incident: Officer turns to his men, looks as many in the eye as possible and says 'Trust me'.
Effect: All units retreat one move!

Smaller battles from the campaign that lend themselves to this level of game include:

Grodno, 1708. During the night of 29 January a Russian brigade-sized force of 3,000 dragoons in three regiments commanded by Brigadier Muhlenfels attacked the Swedish outposts around Grodno. The sentries heard the Russians approach and raised the alarm. During the confused fighting in the suburbs of the town the Swedish advanced guard/garrison of 600 men beat off the attack. These Swedish troops were a combination of the Drabants and elements of the Life Guard of Horse. Fighting in the pitch dark, troops were identifiable only by the language they spoke. In this action, class

the Swedes as Veteran or Elite and the Russians as a mixture of Raw and Trained. For added spice, allow the Russians a supporting gun on a roll of 5 or 6; the Swedes get artillery support on a roll of 4, 5 or 6.

The Russians missed a very real chance of capturing Charles XII, who was asleep in a bed in Grodno when the alarm was raised. Brigadier Muhlenfels was placed under arrest by the Tsar after the raid but escaped and offered his services to the Swedes, where he supplied details of the Russian military position. What could have been a deft political move went horribly wrong when the Swedes lost Poltava – the hapless Brigadier was captured when the Swedes surrendered at Perovolochka and was summarily executed.

Veprik, 1709. On 7 January elements of the Swedish army attempted to capture the Russian outpost at Veprik, a hilltop fort defended by earthen ramparts, which the defenders had turned into walls of ice by pouring water on them. The garrison consisted of a two-battalion Russian regiment supported by about 400 Cossacks (whose few hunting rifles proved of inestimable value during the action).

The Swedish attacking force consisted of six infantry regiments and two dismounted dragoon regiments, 3,000 men in all, commanded by the King himself, accompanied by Field Marshal Rehnskold. The plan was for Swedish artillery to breach the walls prior to an attack by three columns, one attacking each angle of the triangular fort. The attack failed, partly owing to poor artillery preparation (damp powder), partly by lack of coordination, but also because of the murderous fire from the defenders, Cossack marksmen targeting Swedish officers and men carrying storming ladders. In two hours and several attacks, the Swedes lost 400 men killed and 600 wounded, including the Field Marshal. Out of ammunition, the garrison surrendered the next day.

This would lent itself well to a refight, especially with three Swedish players vying to be first to capture the fort. During the action no quarter was expected or given, and the targeting of officers showed that military niceties and conventions had gone out the window. This should be reflected in the scenario, as should the weather (intermittent snow showers and freezing temperatures).

The third redoubt, Poltava, 1709. This scenario

would be somewhat similar to the last, where the third redoubt in the projecting spur of Russian redoubts at Poltava would be attacked by two Swedish regiments, reinforced by a further four regiments, commanded by Major-General Roos. The garrison (one battalion of Russian infantry supported by four regimental guns) held off all Swedish assaults throughout the early morning, the dead piling up on the chevaux de frise around the triangular redoubt or in the surrounding ditch.

The Swedes would be classed as Trained or Veteran; the Russians fought like Veterans, and should be classed as such. (This might have had something to do with the fact that the Swedes took no prisoners during their attacks on the first two redoubts, incentive for any defender.) In the end, Roos pulled his battalions away from the redoubt, and, while the remaining 1,600 men were regrouping, they were attacked by Russian dragoon and infantry formations. This, the fight by Roos and his command, would itself make another excellent refight.

As you can see, this level of wargame can allow more direct involvement by the players in the game by giving due emphasis to the command structure within the battalions fighting, and allows greater input from a devious and sadistic umpire. Other games could include the running fight of Roos and his men through Yakovetski Wood at Poltava, the storming of the Cossack stronghold of Baturin by Menshikov's dragoons, the cavalry assault on the Russian square on the Swedish right wing at Poltava, or even attempts by *ad hoc* Swedish cavalry units to cut through the Russians to rescue isolated infantrymen during the closing stages of the battle.

Full Sized Battles

These games are more straightforward to stage, and any of the main battles of Holowczyn, Lesnaya or Poltava would make an enjoyable gaming scenario. Rules available include *Warfare in the Age of Reason* (Emperor's Press), *The Age of Marlborough* (Gladiator Games), *Wargame Rules for the 1688–1721 Period* (Jessica Productions/Stuart Asquith), *Koenig Krieg*, or rather their Marlburian supplement *La Guerre du Roi* (Barry Grey, sold by Frei Korps), *WRG Napoleonic Rules* (which cover the period from 1700), *18th Century Rules* (Tabletop Games) and

probably several other sets. These all have their advantages and disadvantages, but none of them were designed specifically with the Great Northern war in mind.

The ability of Swedish units to continue functioning long after those of other nations would have been routed or surrendered must be borne in mind. The final Swedish infantry charge would have been an unthinkable action if performed by any other army; Lewenhaupt not only reached the enemy but pushed them back despite tremendous casualties. The same was true of the troops under the control of Roos. Most rules make no concession for Swedish aggression or of their cavalry tactics (squadrons charging in chevron formation). Both the *gå på* tactical doctrine and the impetus of the cavalry chevron give the Swedish player a distinct advantage. This can be countered by a Russian player making the best possible use of firepower to break down the enemy before contact, and using his (often superior) numbers to outflank the opposition.

A number of 'what ifs' could be built into a conventional wargame refight, such as the following.

What if Charles XII was able to take command of his army in person at Poltava? Napoleon's comments regarding the advantage of the moral over the physical mean that the psychological bonus for his army might have allowed the Swedes to win the day.

What if Lewenhaupt and the surviving Swedish troops caught with their backs to the River Dnieper at Perovolochka had chosen to fight? Although cornered and disorganised, they outnumbered their Russian pursuers, and the Swedish army was still a formidable opponent. Lack of discipline meant that surrender was inevitable. What if Charles XII had stayed with his troops and rallied them?

At Holowczyn, what would have happened if the Russians were able to mobilise Sheremetiev's Division to the north and that of Goltz to the south before the Swedes had crossed the river and swamp? Could Repnin's Russians have forced them back or chopped up the Swedish units piecemeal if they had been adequately supported? In launching his attack, Charles was counting on the track-record of passivity in the Russians, hoping they would just stand there and let him run rings around them. What if Repnin were a more aggressive commander? What if Menshikov were on hand to take direct control of the Russian forces?

What if Roos had managed to rejoin the main army before its final attack, increasing the infantry available to Lewenhaupt by 50%? What if Rehnskold had managed to shake the Swedish cavalry down into some form of order before the infantry attack was launched? With their support, the outcome of the battle might well have been different.

One of the delights of wargaming is that you can modify history to try to gain a greater insight into military battles.

Campaign Games

A number of suitable campaign systems are available to anyone wishing to string their battles together and give them more of a purpose. *Koenig Krieg* rules publish a Seven Years War campaign system structured to be run in conjunction with their miniatures rules. Although you would need to draw up a new map for the different theatre of campaign, the system itself could be used. It places due emphasis on the supply problems facing a commander, which could be adapted to reflect the situation in the early eighteenth century in general and eastern Europe in particular. *Warfare in the Age of Reason* includes a Seven Years War campaign system that uses area movement. I have used this (with minor geographical adaptations) to run a Great Northern War campaign.

Whichever system is used, you need to take account of a number of factors particular to the campaign.

The Swedes were fighting hundreds of miles away from friendly territory, their supply bases and any available reinforcements. Consequently, losses could not be replaced. The Russians had a major advantage here.

Supply lines for an army living off the land are irrelevant. If the land has been devastated (Menshikov and his 'scorched earth' tactics), you have real problems. Your army has to move where the available stocks of food are.

The winter of 1708/9 was particularly severe. Any troops not in winter quarters should suffer extremely heavy attrition. If this is tied in with logistical rules where each village can only provide shelter for so many men, then you recreate the historical situation where the Swedes launched attacks on enemy-held villages such as Veprik in order to supply the army with adequate shelter and security from enemy raids.

The diplomatic aspects of the campaign are particularly important during the winter and following spring. What can Charles offer the Cossacks or the Turks to bring them over to his side? Cossack support needs to be factored in, and pre-emptive Russian raids such as those conducted by Menshikov should pay dividends.

A further form of strategic campaigning is available these days: play by mail. Agema Publications run a play by mail campaign entitled *La Gloire du Roi*, 'set in the age of Marlborough, King Louis XIV, Tsar Peter the Great, Charles XII'. A player takes the part of one of the 'enlightened monarchs' or one of their principal subjects and play uses mailed maps, reports and newsletters. Similar organisations such as Flagship have projects for those more into the strategic aspects of early eighteenth century campaigning.

Whichever method is used, the charm of the period should be allowed to shine through the bare bones of the campaigning structure. One final word on campaigns. Many are started; few are finished. If the system is kept simple, playable and still reflects the nature of the period, then you may be on to one that will keep up the momentum once the initial enthusiasm of some of the participants has waned.

Boardgaming

Only two boardgames exist with a Great Northern War theme at the moment, and both were produced by Peter Englund, the author of the Swedish best-seller *Poltava*, now available in English. The first was *Holowczyn (Battle of the Moscow Road)* produced in 1980 by Swedish Game Production. The map measures 39cm by 28cm, with a ground scale of one hexagon representing 160 metres, and each counter representing a battalion or cavalry regiment. The game system penalises the Russian player in the first few turns, to represent the inertia of Repnin. This means that the Swedish player has to go hell for leather at the Russians to take full advantage of the Russian inactivity while he has the chance. If the

Swedish player is in the least bit cautious he will find himself facing an aggressive and numerically superior enemy, and the outcome will be anything but historic.

The second game is *Peter the Great (The defeat of Sweden at Poltava, 1709)*. Produced as an issue game in *The Wargamer* magazine (No. 27) in 1983, the game is an eminently playable refight of the battle. It uses a similar game scale and unit size to Englund's previous game but is altogether a larger and more stylish product. The map measures 65cm by 55cm and the rules have been extended to reflect the storming of redoubts, the use of grenades and the tendency of the Russian foot to stay within their fortified camp for the first half of the battle. Again, the pressure is on the Swedish player to bypass the redoubt line and storm the fortified camp before the numerically superior, but slower-moving, Russian army can crush it.

It has been rumoured that Peter Englund has been working on a new project, a campaign game called *The Road to Moscow*. This will most probably be a strategic study of the whole campaign. Occasional mentions of its development appear in *Strategy and Tactics* magazine, the premier boardgaming journal, but no production date has been confirmed.

Whichever way you choose to wargame the Poltava campaign, it will prove a rewarding and at times frustrating experience. The eighteenth century as a wargaming 'period' is becoming increasingly popular. It is only fair that the momentous events of the Great Northern War are also given due attention. The campaign has everything a wargamer could wish for – colourful uniforms, even more colourful commanders, an interesting variety of weapon and troop types and unusual terrain to fight over. Whether you wish to follow in the footsteps of the Swedish warrior king or Peter the Great, Tsar of all the Russias, remember the sentiment the Swedish tactical doctrine – *Gå På*!